More books by Donna Huston Murray

The Ginger Barnes Main Line Mysteries:
THE MAIN LINE IS MURDER
FINAL ARRANGEMENTS
SCHOOL OF HARD KNOCKS
A SCORE TO SETTLE
FAREWELL PERFORMANCE (e-book pending)
LIE LIKE A RUG
FOR BETTER OR WORSE
Finalist, National Indie Excellence Award, Mysteries

The Lauren Beck Crime Novels:
WHAT DOESN'T KILL YOU
**Hon. Mention 2015 Writer's Digest Self-Published
Book Awards**
GUILT TRIP, The Mystery
**Hon. Mention 2018 Writer's Digest Self-Published
Book Awards**

A Traditional Mystery:
DYING FOR A VACATION

No Bones About It

About It

A Ginger Barnes Main Line Mystery #4

DONNA HUSTON MURRAY

Ravenhill
Press

Cover design by Melissa Williams Design

You are invited to contact the author at:
donnahustonmurray.com

For my #1 son, Casey, who was born wise

Chapter 1

My only choices were a) admit defeat and phone Linda, my dog-trainer friend, or b) try my last idea.

The trouble was, Linda and her ex-husband Karl shared custody of a German shepherd named Tibor, a paragon of a dog who–if you believed his co-owners–could have written the Gettysburg address and delivered it, too. When Linda used him to demonstrate perfection at our beginners' class, the shepherd sneered as if he were Zeus gazing down from Olympus. How embarrassing would it be to confess I can't teach our four-month-old Irish setter to do anything?

Since we were only after that silly Irish setter personality, not a living art object worth hundreds of dollars, after school one day, my son Garry and I answered a local newspaper ad. A Lancaster-County farmer had bred his own two setters. He described them as "hunters" rather than show dogs and priced them accordingly.

Both the man and his wife agreed the puppies' mother possessed a sweet, affectionate disposition, but his father was…husband and wife exchanged a glance. "We almost got rid of him," admitted the woman. One more litter, said the husband's nod. The condition of their living room conveyed that they needed the money. I cheerfully handed it over.

As we drove out of their lane with our new family member snuggled in Garry's lap, Daddy Dog pranced through the rain alongside our car, head held high like the champion he reputedly had been. Surely the glint in his eye was just pleasure over his freedom.

It was.

We named our little darling after the astonishing hockey player Wayne Gretzky, (a.k.a. The Great One), and soon learned he had a prodigious capacity for affection. Unfortunately, he was also a scamp with an irritating sense of humor. Just this afternoon, when I wanted to relax with coffee and the morning paper, he barked at me for half an hour. He did not need to go out. He wasn't hungry. Swatting him produced no effect. Ignoring him? No effect. Gretsky simply wanted to see me jump through hoops for the fun of it.

"Okay," I challenged. "We'll see who's Alpha Dog around here."

I climbed onto the living room coffee table, put my hands on my hips, and barked right back at him.

Gretsky stopped long enough to blink. Then he joined me in a ridiculous duet of opposing wills. I looked and sounded like an idiot, but luckily the kids were at Bryn Derwyn Academy's day camp. My husband Rip was there, too, doing the zillion things headmasters do in the summer.

Since I was obviously an unconvincing Alpha Dog, I gave up. Gretsky kept barking, of course, and for a second, I experienced a pang of nostalgia for our previous Irish setter, Barney.

Barney and I had a rapport. If I so much as thought about walking him, he would shimmy with joy. When the kids' bus was late, he would raise an eyebrow of concern. The morning he bolted for the house next door, I knew for certain there was an emergency involving Letty MacNair, our reclusive older neighbor.

Unfortunately, Barney's heart gave out shortly after that episode. All four of us Barneses cried for days.

We acquired Gretsky more as a diversion than a

replacement. With time and luck, maybe a special rapport would come.

Meanwhile–aspirin. Gretsky had finally run off on his own *silent* mission, so I was free to rummage around in the kitchen junk drawer for two Bayer, which I downed with water straight from the tap.

Should I reach for a lifeline? Linda did say anyone in the beginners' class was free to call about a specific problem, so technically I wouldn't be imposing upon our friendship. Although at the moment Gretsky seemed to be behaving himself.

Wrong. Our Great One scooted past me with something light blue in his mouth and his daddy's glint in his eye.

The little scamp had stolen a pair of my panties. Head throbbing, I set off after him.

We circled the living room coffee table. He zigged when I zagged. I lunged. With four legs to my two, a trot was enough to avoid my grasp.

Prancing like a Lippizaner, he exited the living room and down the hallway past the kids' bedrooms.

"Come on, Gretsky, *give,*" I begged as I lumbered after him.

He glanced back on his way into the added-on family room, where a sofa rose like an island centered in front of the television. I knew he would do laps around it until I fell flat on my face, so after shutting the door behind us, I laid a wooden chair between the back of the sofa and the bookcase.

Gretsky leaped over it.

I extracted a broom from the closet, planning to swipe the dog's hip. Maybe he would slow down enough for me to grab my underwear.

The broom missed the dog's rear by eighteen inches, but Gretsky's eyebrows straightened with dismay. He oozed forward like Secretariat eying the stretch. I vowed never to miss the clothes hamper again.

"Drop it!"

A fast glance and another leap over the chair.

Never mind keeping my sneakers off the upholstery, I climbed over the back of the sofa.

Gretsky faked right and bolted left. From my high position on the seat cushions I thrust the broom in front of the oncoming dog. He stopped just long enough to entice me to the floor. Then he rounded the broom, flew over the chair, and stood with his back to the wall like a gunfighter covering a roomful of enemies.

I flopped onto the sofa, arms folded over my heaving chest, and glared at him while I caught my breath.

Gretsky saw the door had bounced unlatched enough for him to nose his way out.

"Bad dog!" I shouted after him. Wasted breath.

Rubbing the back of my neck, I contemplated the phone resting on an end table. Linda really had invited her students to call anytime.

"I need another private lesson," I confessed after we exchanged hellos.

"Sorry, Gin. I just...no. Sorry."

The strong, assertive woman no dog dared disobey sounded shaken and vulnerable.

"What's wrong?" I asked.

Linda took a slow, ragged breath.

"Karl's dead," she said. "Tibor did it."

Chapter 2

"OH, MY, LINDA! How?" I blurted regarding her shocking news.

"Karl practiced with Tibor every morning."

She slurred her words, and the prickles of apprehension I felt when she first answered the phone returned tenfold. Linda was hypoglycemic, and if she had forgotten to eat...

"I'm afraid I don't understand. Practiced what?" I encouraged, hoping to hear her talk some more.

"Tracking. That was how Tibor got fed." Clearly, she had to concentrate on each word.

Horrible visions of a hungry dog stalking down and killing his master flashed onto my mental screen.

"You're saying Karl always made Tibor find his food that way?" The routine must have had something to do with the unusual sport Karl loved, something starting with an "s." The hobby was the reason he demanded, and received, joint custody of the dog.

"Yesh. In the field behind the trees."

Linda referred to the far back of the property that had once been half hers. Now she lived on an inherited estate in Gladwyne, an especially spacious section of Philadelphia's Main Line. Who got which real estate had been the easiest part of her and Karl's divorce settlement, yet it still took their attorneys a month to negotiate.

"Akeesha said Karl's throat...he wasn't moving, and Tibor had blood on his mouth, his ears, all over. He was growling and circling around Karl's body, and the poor girl was too scared to scream. She just ran."

"Akeesha?" Linda was slurring so badly I wasn't sure I'd heard her correctly.

"Office manager," she clarified, which gave me a

better idea of what might have evolved.

A nutritionist specializing in weight loss, Karl conducted his extensive private practice out of his Chestnut Hill home. When he hadn't appeared for his first appointment, this Akeesha person probably figured he was still out back with his dog. Maybe she waited a few minutes before searching for him, maybe not. Either way, she was in for quite a trauma.

Rather than dwell on such terrible thoughts, I switched my concern to Linda. She had answered my questions well enough, but she sounded increasingly spacey, almost drunk. During the stressful time after her mother died, I knew she'd been hospitalized for neglecting her illness, which was why I asked whether she had eaten.

"Wha'? I dunno."

She hadn't.

Gauging how far her condition had already deteriorated was impossible over the phone. All I knew for certain was she probably wouldn't eat unless some-body stood there and watched her do it.

I told her I'd be right over. After I satisfied myself Linda was on safe ground, I would line up a relative or neighbor to monitor her until she was again ready to monitor herself.

She gulped in a big raspy sob. "He's dead, Gin. He's really dead. All those times I wished it…"

Time for me to get going.

From the kitchen doorway Gretsky watched me extract my keys and hook my purse over my shoulder. His eyes and body seemed to anticipate a reprimand, but for what? I couldn't quite remember.

The setter's deep brown eyes flicked toward a scrap of blue cloth. Ah, the infuriating underwear war.

He's dead. He's really dead I heard Linda mumble in

my memory, and the vast gap between her problem and mine produced such a lump in my throat I had to open my mouth to breathe.

"You keep them for now," I told my dog, and the worry in one small world slipped away. "We'll have a rematch when I get home."

Before I knew better, I'd have supposed summers on Gladwyne's gently rolling lawns were all croquet and lemonade beneath hundred-year-old oaks. Where Rip and I bought, only a few miles away, it was still carpool to Little League and ice cream after. Not that we didn't have lovely hills and trees. We just didn't live in Gladwyne.

And, personally, I didn't care. I'd been living on the "Main Line"—the main line of the old Pennsylvania Railroad—just long enough to know that who lived in which sized house was much more whimsical and random than the stereotypes suggested. Also, everyday human problems were just as prevalent as anywhere else.

Linda happened to live in a rock of a house formerly owned by her mother and her grandmother before her, a gray stone pile softened by apple-green ivy that turns red in the fall. Compared to its neighbors, the surrounding thirty-acre patch of relatively flat turf supported surprisingly few trees, but I liked the airy simplicity of the place. When you were out in the yard for a dog-training class, the sky seemed vast. And now, as the June sun was just beginning to carve sharp edges onto everything in sight, the shade inside the stone arches leading into the house were especially welcoming.

I knocked on the dark-blue door.

No answer.

I was considering whether I should climb through one of the leaded casement windows to rescue Linda when the door creaked open, revealing a wan face with dark hollows under her eyes.

"Linda, it's me, Gin," I alerted her. The shadows seemed to absorb her attention more than me, but she stepped back enough to let me through.

Goose bumps rose on my arms from the chill of the house. Apparently, the small rooms of the previous century had been reconfigured into the more hospitable expanses popular today. Alcoves and other odd-shaped recesses suggested the original charm, but the lightened hardwood floors and red, black, and ivory furnishings transformed the house into a designer's dream.

Linda seemed to be studying my knees.

"Are you all right?" I asked.

She lifted her chin to peer into my face. The crease on her forehead questioned why I was there.

I addressed her the way one would a timid child. "When we spoke on the phone, you said you hadn't eaten, and I remembered..." Linda wasn't listening. "Can I get you something now?"

She stared at the closest end table as if wondering what it was.

I left her to puzzle it out alone and made my way through the long living area into a huge yellow and white kitchen. Eight six-over-six windows on the three rear walls overlooked a patio, the grape arbor, an ancient lilac, and a tennis court.

After a bit of rummaging around, I came up with chocolate milk and a handful of glazed oatmeal cookies to try to repair Linda's body chemistry.

"Here," I said, handing them to her when I returned.

Linda had lowered herself onto the sofa, knees together, hands curled in her lap. She wore a summery, olive green outfit that showed her to be waif-thin. So thin that my okay figure probably looked Junoesque in comparison. Her short, dark-brown curls revealed small, pretty ears and her everyday gold hoop earrings.

I calculated she must have gotten the news about Karl sometime between getting dressed and eating breakfast. As it was now three in the afternoon, she was way overdue for nourishment.

"Come on," I urged. "Drink this."

Linda sipped at the milk.

"All of it," I insisted, like the mother I was.

"Let's go. Atta girl."

She finished the milk then nibbled the first cookie all by herself. Several minutes later she had eaten them all.

I ventured to ask her doctor's name.

"Why?" she inquired, wiping the crumbs from her lips.

"Because I have to ask him, or her, something."

"What?"

I reminded her that the last time she'd had a shock like this she ended up in the hospital. "Since nobody else is here to see whether you lapse into a coma, I need to know if it's okay for me to go home sometime soon."

"Oh, you can. I just have to eat regularly."

"What about your training classes? Do you have any calls to make?"

"Oh, Roxanne, yes. Thanks." She stepped into the kitchen to conduct a brief conversation on the phone, opening with a sketchy something's-come-up-can-you-take-over-the-next-couple-of-classes? with a bit of thanks-for-the-sympathy-but-I-don't-want-to-talk-about-it at the end.

While she took care of business, I reflected about how strange it felt to be there. Linda and I had attended tenth and eleventh grade at Ludwig High School with a few hundred other ordinary suburban kids in a town closer to the shrinking farmland stretching away from Philadelphia than to the city itself.

As a result, the levels of sophistication in our high

school covered a wide range, with a median of about four on a scale of ten. I put myself at three; Linda was at least a nine. I admired her style but lacked her nerve. I suspect she paraded me in front of her parents to delude them into thinking she was clueless as me. She then went out and raised hell, usually leaving me to find my own ride home.

After her family moved up and away from Ludwig, Linda married a nutritionist named Karl Vogel and set herself up as a professional dog trainer. Financially, she never looked back.

I married the wise and winning Robert Ripley Barnes, and we had a daughter and a son. While Rip, initially a private-school English teacher, learned how to run a school, I completed a trial-and-error course on do-it-yourself repairs titled "How to Save Money Or Else." After Rip got hired to head the fledgling Bryn Derwyn Academy, we relocated to the campus, which happened to be on the Main Line.

Buying dog food one day, I noticed Linda's card on the store's counter, realized we once again lived minutes apart, and decided to find out whether we had matured enough to become real friends.

We had not. But we were acquaintances with a history, and that was enough to support a few nostalgic laughs over an endive salad now and then.

I certainly liked Linda well enough not to let her slip into a coma. I did not kid myself that she liked me well enough to accept chocolate milk and oatmeal cookies from me more than once. So before she could hang up, I eased into the kitchen and held out my hand for the phone.

Linda glared, but she did hand it over.

"Roxanne," I said. "This is Gin Barnes, an old friend of Linda's." In the interest of expediency, I pressed the issue. "Something really disturbing…"

Linda's hand flew up in a stop-sign gesture, and her

scowl hardened.

"…a family problem came up; and it might be a good idea if somebody checks whether Linda is eating regularly. Can you do it?"

Roxanne didn't live close enough, but she told me the name of another part-time assistant who did. She also agreed to call the person and explain.

"You always were the motherly sort," Linda remarked.

"Thank you," I said. We were both smiling.

"Is there anything else you don't want me to do before I go home and get out of your life?"

She actually laughed, and I experienced a fleeting memory of all the faces of all the people my mother helped over the years—after the faces melted with acceptance. Cynthia Struve was a woman of convictions, annoying and interfering as those convictions were. Catching myself behaving just like her gave me the shivers.

"You going to be all right now?" I asked as we eased back into the living room.

"Sure. It was just such a shock. And Tibor, I'm awfully upset about Tibor." Her brow clouded over again, and she had to bite her lip to keep it from trembling.

And I finally realized how I would feel if a dog I trusted and loved turned vicious.

A knock at the door ended my moment of empathy. Linda rolled her eyes toward the ceiling and offered an apologetic "What now?" smile. Then she walked swiftly and surely to the door,

Minding my manners, I waited by the sofa while she greeted her next guest.

Except it wasn't a concerned friend or neighbor. It was two uniformed police officers.

The one in charge asked whether Linda was indeed

the former wife of Dr. Karl A. Vogel.

She admitted she was.

The officer nodded grimly. Then he began to read from the card he held in his palm.

"You have the right to remain silent..."

Chapter 3

THE OFFICER finished the last line, asked if Linda understood her rights, glanced briefly at me, then addressed her once again. "You're being arrested for the murder of Karl A. Vogel."

"But I was here, right here, all morning!" she stated.

Watching Linda's profile, I tried hard to catch more evidence of indignation or shock. Anything but mild consternation.

She told the men she would get her purse.

That was it? How could she allow herself to be escorted to jail so easily?

"But you didn't..." I objected for her. "You couldn't have. You said you were here."

"Yes."

"Tell them again," I urged, jerking a thumb at the arresting officers.

"I'm supposed to keep quiet." The Miranda warning.

"You can, but you don't have to." I couldn't believe this was the woman I'd heard berate a miniature poodle who refused to heel, the woman who finessed 120-pound Newfoundlands into compliance. Had the divorce undermined her confidence so totally? Had Karl? Could her blood sugar level possibly be that low?

Watching her make her way across the room, collect her purse, then retrace her steps, I concluded it must be a combination of all three. *Unless she knew a big-shot lawyer who would clear up the problem in a hurry.*

"It'll be all right," she told me as she passed by, so maybe she did know a big-shot lawyer.

At the door she turned back to coolly ask me to lock up her house.

Back home I went through the motions of starting

dinner, but all I thought about was Karl's horrific death, Linda's arrest, and how suddenly tragedy can wreck a person's life.

Gretsky eyed me with concern from his favorite sun spot; and when at last I dried my hands, I joined him on the braided rug for a comforting snuggle.

Tears of frustration and fatigue led me to think about my mother. How she believed in doing what needed to be done simply to put things right with herself.

I also considered Linda's hasty arrest. She was a professional dog trainer, true, but didn't that mean she would never ever turn a family pet into a lethal weapon? The thrust of her whole career was to domesticate dogs, to make them loving and loveable companions. With all the other methods of mayhem available, if she actually intended to kill Karl, she would have chosen another way. Using a dog she loved simply wouldn't occur to her.

I sniffed and wiped my eyes on my sleeve and sat upright. Then I made my way into the family room to turn on the TV. It was after five. Maybe I could catch the local news before Rip and the kids got home.

As expected, the news director used the sensational item as a teaser. "…shocking death of a prominent diet doctor when his own dog turned on him. More after this…"

I endured a bunch of commercials, the daily car crash item, the daily fire-somewhere-around-here item, the pressing question of how many of the city's fountains would be turned on this summer (of most interest to the homeless who bathed in them). Then the camera finally switched to Karl's front lawn where a reporter wearing a wheat-colored jacket and hot-pink tie lowered his eyebrows to confide to his greater-Philadelphia audience.

"This morning a German shepherd trained to attack assailants apparently turned on his master. Dr. Karl A.

Vogel, the prominent diet doctor, was an enthusiast of the sport called 'schutzhund,' which when translated means 'protection dog.' His own pet, Tibor von Toten haus, is a third-level schutzhund champion, but today something went horribly wrong."

Our front screen door slammed, and Garrett Ripley Barnes shouted, "Hi, Gretsky, ole dog, ole buddy."

Simultaneously, the newsman reported, "Instead of following the usual commands to track his owner's footsteps to where his food had been placed, the German shepherd went berserk, attacked Dr. Vogel, and killed him."

Our front door slammed again, followed by "Hi, Mom." "Hi, honey."

"Quiet!" I shouted with one ear cocked to the TV.

"The police are questioning the victim's ex-wife and Tibor's co-owner, Linda Arden, regarding the matter. Ms. Arden is a well-known dog trainer, having won many obedience ribbons with the same dog that attacked Dr. Vogel."

The "questioning" part wasn't quite accurate, but for once I was glad they'd hedged on the facts.

Framed by the doorjamb, Robert Ripley Barnes tugged at his red tie. Observing me from beneath a shock of straight brown hair that forever tumbled forward, his smile gave way to concern.

"Something wrong?" he asked, setting aside the folder of work he'd brought home.

"News. Never mind. It's over." I turned off the set.

"What happened?" He sank down beside me, and I noticed his socks were smeared with mud.

I told him about Karl. And about Linda.

"Wow. Must be some pretty compelling evidence against her."

"You'd think so, wouldn't you?" The authorities, ever

conscious of the cost of a false arrest, would never have acted so decisively without evidence. "But she wasn't on the scene, so what proof could there be?"

Rip patted my thigh. "Let's eat before Garry starts on the woodwork." At age eleven our son was contemplating a growth spurt, if the quantity of food he devoured was any indication—hence the family nickname, "Termite." Chelsea, age thirteen, was a wealth of conflicting diet information all gleaned from the Internet and gossip. Consequently, her eating habits were less predictable than the weather.

"How's the gym coming along?" I asked my husband as we settled around the plank table for our meal. The expensive project had been a surprise fundraising headache bequeathed by Rip's predecessor and Bryn Derwyn's attorney, Richard Wharton, a troublesome guy who managed to get himself murdered in the school's community room. The fallout from that disaster nearly closed the small, private school, which would have put its new Head out of a job and his family out on the street.

"First rows of cement block today," Headmaster Barnes proudly announced. His green eyes sparkled like a boy with a new box of Legos. The biggest set.

"That explains the mud," I remarked.

"What? Oh, yes." His head bobbed in agreement.

My hope was for Rip's Christmas-morning smile to last all summer. Then, if the off-season problems that cropped up at school were small enough, Bryn Derwyn's Fearless Leader might face September with his batteries recharged and ready. If the summer proved to be tough, it would be a long, weary winter.

"And how's camp?" I asked our kids.

"Ms. Hepple went home sick," Chelsea announced with a mixture of amazement and regret. "I had all seven six-year-olds by myself for three hours."

Bryn Derwyn ran a small-scale day camp of the old-fashioned, all-round variety. Swimming, various other sports, arts and crafts, nature study. As a three-year veteran, Chelsea was now a Counselor-in-Training. Garry was an older camper, and not too happy about it. Yet he stayed on while his sister earned extra money babysitting the late pickups, so apparently he didn't mind too much.

I glanced at Rip.

"Appendicitis," he answered my unasked question about the counselor. "She had surgery this afternoon. Out for two weeks."

"Oh, no," Chelsea moaned.

"She's fine," Rip assured her. "And I'm already asking around about a temporary nature counselor, so you can stop playing Camille."

Chelsea gave a humorous groan of relief before switching her attention to her spaghetti.

Garry held his plate out for more.

I gauged the camp's personnel problem to be too short-term to ruin my husband's summer. However, it just might ruin mine. Chelsea was okay with little kids, better than okay probably, but two weeks of seven-hour days? Not even professional daycare specialists did that to themselves.

"How about tomorrow?" I inquired.

"You volunteering?" Rip asked with a crooked smile. He knew my weaknesses and wasn't above using his knowledge. "Haven't rushed in to solve enough problems this week?"

I threw up both hands. "Completed my row of stars today," I said in my own defense.

Rip spun a forkful of pasta, paid attention to anything but me.

In about two minutes I crumbled.

"So what about tomorrow?" I asked again.

"Field trip to Goodwin's Dairy Farm. Plenty of mothers going. You're off the hook."

"Phew," I said, pretending to wipe sweat from my brow.

Rip laughed.

After the dinner dishes were cleared up and the kids went off for showers and TV, Rip and I took our iced tea out back to the lawn chairs. Robins indulged themselves in their loud twilight peep, and the pleasant sound of neighborhood children playing reached our ears through the shrubbery.

"Linda really had to be hospitalized after her mom died?" Rip remarked.

"Oh, yeah. She passed out in the church."

"And you knew just talking to her she was in trouble?"

"Well, yeah," I replied, but then my mind went off on its own. "You think the police are making sure she eats?"

"Probably not." Rip settled back and gazed at the fading sky.

I began to twitch. He was right. The police would have no interest in how much Linda ate or when, and today proved she was incapable of monitoring herself when she was under duress.

"I'll just call in the morning and see if she's all right," I concluded out loud.

"I knew it," Rip crowed, clapping his hands together, then glancing at his watch. "Less than half an hour. You really are Cynthia's daughter."

I punched his arm. Playfully, of course.

"Ouch," he complained. "That was a compliment."

"Doesn't matter. You tricked me."

"Into what? Admitting to what you were going to do anyway? Sorry, Gin. You're a nice person. Get over it."

I had absolutely no idea how to respond to that.

Chapter 4

IN THE MORNING I dressed for the grocery store rather than the police station, sneakers rather than flats, and an embroidered denim vest over my white shirt and jeans because the air conditioning at my store is frigid. It was my way of promising myself to check on Linda's welfare, then to go about my own business. Rip's remarks about my Cynthia-like habits had hit home.

The local police station was of the low-budget, low-maintenance variety. A one-story, new brick structure with a flat roof, a tidy yard with little red and yellow marigolds at the base of the flagpole, and a parking lot for about thirty cars, it seemed to wait quietly in the June sun for something significant to happen. The mail delivery perhaps.

Inside was only slightly more active. Half a dozen men and women in uniforms or civilian clothes moved about doing their Wednesday-morning business. At such an early hour they were mostly concerned with speaking on the phone and drinking coffee.

I approached the desk clerk closest to the door. "I'm a friend of Linda Arden, and I just stopped by to see if she's okay."

"Hey, Gin Barnes, isn't it?" a voice called from halfway along a row of desks. Spotting the speaker caused one of those sinking, sorry feeling you get when someone reminds you of a bad time.

The voice belonged to Sergent Detective Kriebel, who had responded to the 911 call when my neighbor Liz Kelman had been mugged. As he approached the front desk where I stood, I noticed his hearty greeting had an underlying skeptical/serious quality, a sort of facial what-are-you-doing-here? accusation. Of course, the few times we spoke about Liz's case he'd been polite, suspicious, condescending, and irritable all at once. That my theory about her death proved to be correct probably didn't endear me to the man.

"Anything I can do?" he asked, wiggling his fingers to dismiss the woman minding the desk. She narrowed her eyes but pushed back her chair and sidled over toward the coffee machine.

"Sure, why not?" I answered. "I came to see how Linda Arden's doing."

"Friend of yours?" Kriebel asked. His clean-shaven face still looked impossibly young beneath pale brown hair. The blue-black uniform slacks were as perfectly pressed as ever, but his short-sleeved uniform shirt revealed winter-white arms dotted with little brown spots. The muscles weren't anything to brag about, but the flint in the man's hazel eyes made up for any perceived weaknesses.

"Yes. More or less," I answered. More her friend than you are. "I know her well enough to know she's hypoglycemic and doesn't take care of herself when she's under stress. Like now."

"Well, I'm sure it's very kind of you to inquire about Ms. Arden's health, but we're responsible for that right now..." The rest of the sentence was an unstated. "So why don't you run along and play in somebody else's yard?"

"She collapsed during her mother's funeral—I was there—so how about humoring me and checking on her condition this morning? If she's okay, I promise I won't bother you again."

Kriebel sighed, torn between serving the public interest his way and mollifying me. He must have decided I was part of the public, too, for he picked up a phone and told whoever was on the switchboard to connect him to a nearby prison.

"She's there?" I asked with alarm.

He covered the mouthpiece with his hand. "We don't have an overnight lockup here."

After a short wait, Kriebel began explaining to someone on the other end. "Friend of Ms. Arden's wants to know if she ate her breakfast."

I held out my hand for the phone. Kriebel pulled a face and glumly relinquished the instrument.

"She's hypoglycemic," I said. "She goes into a coma if she doesn't eat at regular intervals, and if she's under stress she withdraws and forgets to take care of herself."

"We can't make her eat if she doesn't want to," a reasonable-sounding male voice told me.

"Does that mean she hasn't been eating?"

"I'm not sayin' that," the man replied. "All I'm sayin' is…"

I handed the phone back to Kriebel, who hung up without saying good-bye.

"How can she get out of there?" I asked.

"Post bail."

"She have a lawyer?"

"Court-appointed."

I imagined an overworked do-gooder just out of law school with no discernible people skills. Linda had been difficult enough for me to befriend, and I'd been trying. It would be impossible for an underpaid attorney to learn how to connect with her in time to mount a successful defense.

Then another thought occurred to me.

"Does her father know she's there?" I asked.

Kriebel was resting against the desk with his arms spread like a tripod. From this bent-over position he squinted up at me and shrugged. Mr. Warmth.

I skipped the grocery store and drove home. Linda's elderly dad lived somewhere in Florida, and if she had settled for a court-appointed attorney, it was a good bet she hadn't alerted him to her predicament. If the Honorable Kenneth Arden, retired, still drew breath, he would have called out the troops to save his little girl. When we were teenagers, my main function in Linda's eyes had been to perpetuate Daddy's glowing image of her. I had been so naive and so in awe of Linda's sophistication that I considered the whole routine amusing.

Naturally, I lost track of both father and daughter when the family relocated to the Main Line after our junior year of high school.

However, my mother probably knew how to reach the retired judge. Cynthia Struve keeps a ridiculously extensive mailing list. Getting on it means you met her. Getting off it means you died.

She answered her phone on the third ring.

"Hello?" Mother asked.

"Hi, Mom. It's me."

"Yes, dear. What can I do for you? I'm baking English muffins." That meant she was up to her elbows in flour and dough, and she wanted to finish focusing on the instructions before she got confused and had to start over. She wasn't senile—not yet anyway—just easily distracted.

I went straight to the point. "Do you have Linda Arden's father's current address?"

"Kenneth Arden from Ludwig?" Nobody really left Ludwig to my mother's mind. "Certainly," she said as if people frequently called to make use of her mailing list.

"Oh, dear, now I'm going to get my address book all sticky. Hold on." She set down the phone and was off the line for a few minutes.

When she returned, she carefully pronounced every number and word of Kenneth Arden's condo address in

Boca Raton. "You want his phone number?"

"You have it?" I asked with genuine surprise. It had always been my father who revered Judge Arden, reading news items about his esteemed friend at the dinner table and essentially boring Mother and me with every turn of the man's career. With Dad gone, I couldn't imagine my mother having any reason to speak to Linda's father at all.

Then again, my mother and the retired judge were both widowed, and I had to admit a remarkable number of marriages take place in retirement-home chapels. Nothing ventured, nothing gained.

Cynthia gave me the number. "Tell him I said hi," she suggested with a youthful lilt.

"You bet," I assured her. She could do worse than a retired judge.

Fortunately, she was still too preoccupied with her muffins to ask me why I needed his number.

A musical female voice answered the elderly judge's phone.

"This is Ginger Struve Barnes calling. Is Judge Arden available?" I asked.

"He's resting. Is there anything I can help you with?"

"This is really quite important—it concerns his daughter. Are you sure he can't come to the phone for a minute?"

"He's had heart attacks—two heart attacks—and he really shouldn't be bothered. Maybe if you told me, I could…"

"Dolly!" said a third party. "Hang up the phone. I'll take it."

The woman harrumphed but obediently replaced her receiver.

"My nurse," Kenneth Arden said apologetically. "Thinks she's my keeper."

"But the heart attacks…?"

"Ancient history. Now, Ginger Barnes, what's this about my Linnie?"

I sighed. This wasn't going to be easy. "There's been a tragic accident—to her ex-husband," I hastily added. "Tibor, their dog, turned on him." I gulped and forged ahead. "For some reason the police suspect Linda might have had something to do with Karl's death. It's really just a terrible misunderstanding."

"Has she been arraigned?"

For a minute I had forgotten the man had been a judge, a mistake I wouldn't make again.

"Possibly." Probably. "What you should know is Linda isn't putting up a fight. Whether it's the hypoglycemia or shock, I don't know. But she's settled for a court-appointed lawyer." I stopped speaking because I had run out of things to say. It certainly was not the time to relate my mother's cheery hello.

We exchanged silence for half a minute. Then Linda's father instructed me to start at the beginning.

I gave him every detail I knew, nothing more, but nothing less.

"And you have no idea what the evidence against her might be?"

"Other than the fact that she's a dog trainer and had regular access to Tibor, no. I'm really just on the fringes," I reminded him.

He grunted to indicate he understood.

"I'll be calling Timothy Bedoes. Excellent attorney. Young, but savvy. Yes, Timothy Bedoes." The old judge seemed to be tiring, and I was worried about keeping him on the phone any longer. Yet when I began to say good-bye, he spoke my name to keep me on.

"Your father and I were friends, good friends," he said with an emphasis I was meant to take to heart. "I've always regretted I wasn't more help with the union problem he had the year he died."

"That last construction job?" I asked. One of the reasons my father loved teaching high school was the opportunity to work at something completely different each summer. He claimed it kept him young; and perhaps it did—right up until his one and only aneurysm.

"Yes. I tried to advise him, but..."

But suddenly the fact that unions had been harassing his company's work site no longer mattered. I had been in junior high back then . Our fathers' friendship was how I met Linda.

Apparently Judge Arden's thoughts shadowed my own. After another silence, he said, "You've always been good to my Linnie. Oh, I knew you weren't especially close, but I always thought you were good for each other." His voice seemed to break. "Stick with her, Ginny. I wouldn't ask if I could be there myself."

A lump had established itself in my throat. "I'll do what I can," I waffled.

Judge Arden sighed so profoundly you'd have thought I just saved his life.

Chapter 5

I HAD LET Gretsky out into the fenced part of our back yard before I phoned Linda's father in Florida. Now it was four hours later, and I needed him inside so I could finally go to the grocery store.

"Gretsky, come," I shouted out the family-room door. *"Please,"* I added under my breath, but he scarcely gave me a glance.

I offered him a dog biscuit from the decorative jar next to the flour canister. "Cookie?" I coaxed.

No, thanks, he smiled from the broad tree stump he used as a perch, his tail fanning back and forth.

I began to grind my teeth and mutter.

The phone rang.

"Ms. Barnes?" asked a male voice with an urgent if not commanding undertone.

"Yes?" I asked in return.

"Timothy Bedoes calling. Judge Arden engaged my services on behalf of his daughter. I understand you and Linda are good friends?" He was either attempting to be tactful against his nature, or he wasn't very sure of his facts.

"Not very good friends, no," I said.

That surprised the young attorney enough to interrupt the flow of his pre-planned speech. "But you were with Ms. Arden when she was arrested. You called her father. I was led to believe you were the best of friends."

"That's stretching it a little." To say the least.

A heavy sigh reached my ear through the telephone. "But you are willing to help, aren't you? I mean, she needs you. I was hoping you'd be able to come right over."

Why? Was Linda sick? Suicidal? What?

"She's home?" I asked.

"Yes. I'm there now. But I can't stay, and she shouldn't be alone. The judge assured me you agreed to help."

I sighed, feeling the tug of obligation Judge Arden meant me to feel, my conscience listening to the argument the old man had been too proud to state out loud.

Never mind that Linda and I weren't exactly close; our fathers had been. All those boring news clippings about the judge's career—if I got anything out of them, it was how much Donald Struve admired and revered Kenneth Arden.

And apparently relied on him, too, as the man himself so judiciously pointed out. At the time I thought it a curious thing to mention that Dad had turned to the judge for advice as late as the summer he died, especially considering the meeting had been fruitless and the question had very soon become moot.

And yet if I knew anything about Judge Arden it was that his mind was intact. He might be older and physically frail, but he was not prone to self-indulgent ramblings, not considering the way he had elicited every detail of Linda's predicament from me.

So the digression meant something.

Actually everything, as I suddenly realized. Standing there with the kitchen phone in my hand, I visualized exactly what the judge meant me to see—my father, a huge, vibrant man with defiantly reddish hair and granite features summoning up the courage to confide in someone else, to ask for advice. The picture was so unlikely as to be almost unimaginable. And yet I knew it had happened. Whether the phenomenon was regular or rare mattered not one whit. Even when you're strong, sometimes you need the help of someone stronger.

"Honestly," Timothy Bedoes concluded, "there isn't

anyone else to call."

Okay, so maybe I could overlook this guy's irritating presumptions and his time-is-money brevity and think about Linda for a minute.

Think about the idea that maybe her superficial crowd had all grown up and slipped away, leaving her with me as the unqualified, unwilling facsimile of a good friend. If that was even close to true, I felt genuinely sorry for her. Even sorry enough to allow an irritating, presumptuous lawyer to summon me to Linda's side on no notice.

And, of course, I did wonder why she needed the company. If she wasn't in the hospital by now, someone must have made certain she ate.

Could she possibly be in mourning over Karl? Hard to believe, but stranger things have happened.

"I'll be right over," I told Bedoes. As soon as I got my dog to come in.

"Thank you. I'll wait, but I really have to get back to the office."

After we hung up, I contemplated my household dilemma. Gretsky came in for very few reasons: a) Somebody arrived who needed to be greeted, b) He got invited for a ride in the car, or c) He felt like coming in because it was raining or because some obscure portion of his brain told him it was time for a nap. None of the above applied just now.

Desperate times called for desperate measures. I selected a tennis ball from the oval basket on the family-room floor. Then I stepped out into Gretsky's yard and threw him a lob, a grounder, another–nirvana. Nirvana!

The fourth time he retrieved the ball I grabbed the ring of his nylon choke collar and instructed him to heel. He flashed me a sharp look, but the Davy Crockett of dogs finally allowed himself to be led all the way into the fort.

Twenty minutes later I pulled into Linda's drive.

His suit jacket slung over his shoulder in preparation for a hasty departure, Timothy Bedoes rushed out the arched blue door of Linda's stone house the second he heard my tires on the gravel driveway. In honor of the seventy-degree afternoon he had rolled the sleeves of his starched white shirt away from his thin wrists. We met midway along the stone walkway.

"Thank you for coming," he said instead of the what-took-you-so-long? written on his face.

"No problem," I replied as if I meant it.

Bedoes was somewhere between thirty-five and forty, not much older than me. Fair and balding, he swept his medium-blond hair back in a frank, no-vanity-here manner. Unobtrusive glasses slipped down his small nose, and his puffy lips seemed hard-pressed to cover his large, widely gapped teeth.

A massive maple tree dappled us and our surroundings with patches of shade. A breeze fragrant with new-mown grass wafted by. Bedoes gazed into the distance, either enjoying the sense of broad open space or indulging in a breather after the intense effort of getting Linda released on bail.

"There are a few things you should know before you go in there," he began. Then he paused to contemplate some untrimmed growth at the base of the maple before looking me in the eye. "Linda wrote an incriminating letter. It arrived at Karl's house yesterday."

Her attorney monitored my reaction, a narrowing of my lips and a glance at the sky; then he wagged his head, perhaps over human folly.

"Now I know and you know that if she had been training Tibor to attack her ex-husband, she wouldn't have been stupid enough to telegraph her intentions on paper." He raised an index finger to point to the obvious. "But the police can't consider common sense. They have to stick to the facts. Which means the case goes forward; such as it is."

"What did the letter say?" I inquired.

Bedoes folded his jacket over his left arm and regarded me, concerned-person-to-concerned-person, which prompted me to reassess him. Maybe he wasn't cold; maybe he was an excellent lawyer who, consequently, was just plain busy.

"'Never again, Karl,'" the attorney recited. "'You better start looking over your shoulder. I'm going to see to it that you're sorry.'"

"Did Linda tell you exactly what she meant?"

Bedoes shrugged. "Karl pulled a deal that cheated her out of a hundred and twenty-five grand. He lost money, too, incidentally, but Linda thinks he was spiting her. She said she intended to sic the IRS on him."

I grunted.

Bedoes nodded. "Bad luck, huh? Lesson to us all— never put it in writing."

"So why am I here? She can't be very upset by his death."

"Oh, no. You're wrong." The attorney kicked at some grass cuttings on the walkway with a wing-tipped toe, then he once again met my eyes. "She's a wreck. Denial. Guilt. If she hadn't written the letter, she might have been all right. But she wrote it, and now she feels guilty as hell. She needs all the support we can give her."

"I've got kids coming home at five," I remarked.

Bedoes waved a hand as if to say, "Oh, that."

"No worries," he said. "Any show of support will do right now. It's the other I'm counting on, that the judge is counting on."

Now I was seriously perplexed. "What other?"

"He didn't ask you?"

"Ask what?" Now I was getting a bit peeved.

"Judge Arden said you were excellent at making discreet inquiries, finding out what's what without drawing attention to the questions. He assured me you had agreed to be his eyes and ears."

Stick with her, Linda's father had begged. *I'll do whatever I can,* I had replied.

The question was: How did a retired, unwell, ex-judge living in Florida who had been out of contact with me since I was in the eleventh grade have any idea what I'd been doing lately?

Of course: Cynthia had kept him up-to-date.

My anger was volcanic. "Dammit, Mom, this is not *The Dating Game,"* came to mind, as well as a few vociferous complaints. However, they would all have to wait.

After taking a moment to breathe, I told Bedoes, "There's something you and the judge haven't considered."

The attorney raised an eyebrow.

"Linda doesn't especially like me," I said, "and I really doubt she wants my help."

Bedoes shook his head as if I was missing the point. "No, no. You're wrong there. Linda's thought processes aren't working in a linear fashion. Her ex-husband died a horrible death. People think they wish that on people they hate, but it isn't true. She's feeling guilty. We have simply got to help her see she needs us. You must care a little or you wouldn't have phoned her father."

"I don't know."

"The judge specifically requested your involvement. He doesn't want anyone else."

"I think I need to speak with him again."

"He's not really well, you know. Despite what he tells you."

I had a cell phone; I could call Kenneth Arden before I took one step further into his daughter's life. The trouble was I already knew what he would say—and what it would cost the proud old man. "Please," can be a very expensive word.

And yet I was certain neither Linda's father, nor her attorney, knew what they were asking.

"Tim, if you don't mind my calling you Tim," I said, and he responded by giving me his complete attention. "I'm pretty sure Linda's annoyed that I've done as much as I have."

Bedoes gestured toward the door. "Go in. Decide for yourself. But don't forget what I've said."

"Okay," I acceded with little conviction. I waved a foot back and forth before I strode boldly forward.

Bedoes chuckled and headed for his car. His shoulders dipped as each leg touched the ground. Not quite a swagger, his stride didn't exactly say "aw-shucks" either.

As soon as I was inside her house, Linda shouted, "You had a lot of nerve calling my father." She'd been pacing in front of the long red sofa facing the fireplace, but she whirled to a halt to fling her anger at me.

"You'd rather be in jail?" I suggested.

"Miss Goodie Two-Shoes strikes again. Is that it?" She had on the same olive-green outfit from yesterday, except now it was crushed and in serious need of dry cleaning.

I sighed and rested my hands on the back of a wooden chair. "We're a bit more than we were in eleventh grade," I remarked. *And a bit less.* "So how about sparing me the psychological side trips? Is there anything you want? Because I need to get home to my kids pretty soon."

Linda abruptly sat on the sofa. Her hands raked through her curly dark hair and held. The tension made her eyes slant.

"I *wanted* Karl dead, and now he is." She released her hair and looked at me. "Do you think if you wish something hard enough, it can come true?"

I told her I tried that once for a football game. "Didn't work," I hastily added. Now that we were actually holding a conversation, I sat down, too.

"Yeah, but I *really* wanted Karl dead, Gin. I *prayed* for it."

Just as I had prayed for our high school team to win—until I realized the visiting grandstands almost certainly contained somebody praying for the opposite result.

"Stop beating yourself up," I told Linda. "You didn't program Tibor to turn on Karl," and then I had a thought. "Did you?"

"No," she spat at me, and I gratefully scrambled back into presumption-of-innocence mode. Even one moment of doubt had been like dipping my toe into filthy water.

Talking seemed to dilute Linda's ire. Tension maintained its grip on her body, but her emotions leaked through.

"I thought I hated him, Gin," she admitted with a fist quivering in front of her teeth. "And I can't believe he's really gone. Can you beat that?"

If we actually had been good friends, I'd have gone to her side and wrapped my arm around her shoulders. She could have cried into my mauve T-shirt until it looked tie-dyed. But this was just Linda and me, so I said, "Is there anything I can do?"

Linda cried silently for a minute.

"I'm really worried about Tibor," she admitted. "I can't have any contact with him," she laughed through her tears, "as if I might un-brainwash the dog by whispering into his ear." She shook her head. "I'm afraid of what they'll do to him, Gin."

My connection to my children is permanent. No matter where they are or where I am, they can shift to the front and center of my attention within a blink. I believed this to be normal, that we were meant to care for someone or something beyond ourselves.

That is also why I believe people without children sometimes redirect those strong parental inclinations onto their pets. If the anguish on Linda's face was any indication, my theory certainly held true for her.

My sympathy was as genuine as it was powerful. My mind refused to imagine Chelsea or Garry in dire peril, but Linda's face showed me what the unimaginable felt like.

"I'll see what I can find out," I promised.

I could almost feel Timothy Bedoes chalking up another point on the scoreboard of his day.

Chapter 6

FOR SENSITIVE phone calls I preferred the phone on the end table in our living room at the back of the house. The blue plaid sofa, distressed pine coffee table, and walk-in fireplace offered just the homey reassurances such conversations required. For visual escape, two sliding doors opened to our small patio and a view of iris leaves, a lilac long ago picked out of reach, and—between a beech and a couple of mature oaks—a patch of sky.

The Philadelphia police, who had jurisdiction over Karl's death, told me the Pennsylvania Society for the Prevention of Cruelty to Animals was under contract to help them with animal-related cases, and that Tibor was being kept at the organization's Erie Avenue location.

While Alice, the helpful woman who took my call at the PSPCA, informed me Tibor was presently housed in a row of kennels with other "bite cases," my eyes kept seeking out that distant patch of sky.

"His shots are up to date," she added, "so he'll be quarantined here for ten days until we're sure there's no sign of rabies."

Confused, I said, "Wait a minute. Tibor's had his shots, but he still has to be quarantined?"

"The only other way to be positive he doesn't have rabies would be to examine his brain--posthumously."

"Oh." For the time being Tibor would stay put. "What happens after the ten days?" I asked.

"That's up to a judge. Normally, the dog can be returned to the owner, unless it was the owner who trained the dog to bite. Then we would probably have to destroy the dog."

To me, Tibor had always been a coveted object which Karl and Linda used to torment each other. Now it appeared he had been even more sorely used. In one way or another, his handling by our supposedly superior species was responsible for his vicious response. I wasn't especially fond of the dog, but I didn't relish him paying with his life for something that was essentially not his fault.

The irony of my conclusion widened my eyes and dropped my chin: how I felt about Tibor was also exactly how I felt about Linda.

To Alice I said, "In Tibor's case it'll probably take a trial to decide whether Ms. Arden had anything to do with her husband's death, which will take months. Will you keep the dog all that time?"

"I don't know. His case is quite unusual, which is why I say his fate is really up to a judge."

As Tibor's situation sounded gloomier and gloomier, my gaze had shrunk back from the clouds to the lilac leaves to the smudge from Gretsky's nose on the glass door. In desperation I asked, "How about if somebody could prove it wasn't Ms. Arden's fault, then would she get Tibor back?"

Alice hummed thoughtfully across the line. "Like if the training Dr. Vogel was doing with Tibor was the reason the dog turned on him?"

"Yes!" I had been feeling around in the dark, but Alice had reached the light switch first. Although I knew very little about schutzhund training, I did know protection work was part of it.

"Interesting idea," the PSPCA employee reflected. "Of course, for Tibor's sake you'd better get your evidence together before next Friday."

I immediately called Linda to assure her Tibor was safe at the PSPCA but, like any other bite case, he was being quarantined for ten days. I did not elaborate, and Linda did not press me for more information. She needed to hear some good news too badly for either of us to spoil it with unwelcome details.

While I had her on the phone, I asked where Karl's schutzhund club practiced; she once mentioned she couldn't conduct obedience classes on Wednesday nights because Tibor was with Karl at schutzhund.

Naturally, she wanted to know why I asked.

"I'd like to see for myself whether Tibor's protection training might have backfired."

Linda grunted. "Suit yourself," she said, conveying clearly that I was free to waste my time. Her cynicism made me realize how lucky she was Timothy Bedoes brought his own enthusiasm to her defense; she certainly wasn't adding any of her own.

The Delaware Valley Schutzhund Club met at six p.m. at a field about ten minutes from our home. Although I invited my whole family to come watch, only Garry was interested.

Frankly, I was relieved. Our daughter was far too impressionable, and Rip was inclined to be a bit judgmental. I wasn't entirely sure Garry would like what he would see, but offering him something different to do seemed preferable to over-sheltering him.

As it turned out, bringing my son along was the best thing I could have done—for my purposes, at least.

The group practiced at a remote field down an obscure road at a far corner of Valley Forge Park. Trees rimmed the left edge and the back length of the grassy rectangle while paved road bounded the other two sides. About ten vehicles of the boxy dog-crate-toting variety were scattered in the lot next to what appeared to be maintenance buildings.

Garry popped out of the car and rushed over to two German shepherd puppies romping under the shade of a dogwood tree. Down in a crouch, the owner's neck straightened with surprise, as if Garry had dropped off one of the tree's branches. I had no choice but to introduce both myself and my son.

"Linda Arden asked me to do whatever I can for Tibor," I added to explain our presence, "and I thought if I learned something about schutzhund it might help."

The man, whose name was Monk Keller, peered at me from beneath sandy eyebrows. The strength in his slender arms probably didn't depend upon regular visits to a gym. His hand, when he rose to shake mine, was dusty-dry from rubbing puppies who had been playing in the dirt.

"Help yourself," he said, and my eyes followed his sweeping gesture to the people training their dogs out in the field.

There, two well-spaced couples and a single woman were working with two shepherds and a rottweiler. With subtle differences they seemed to be doing the same obedience exercises I'd seen Linda's advanced classes practice–jumping a six-foot A-frame to retrieve a barbell, heeling, sitting, flopping down the instant a firm command was received. Except the commands didn't sound like English.

"Plots?" I asked Monk hoping for a clarification.

"Platz," he said. "Means 'place' in German. We use it for our down command."

"Don't you have to say the dog's name first?" I asked. It had been the first thing we had learned in Linda's class.

"The dog's supposed to be paying attention already."

Oh, I thought. Oh, ho.

"Hup," shouted a man with a moustache, and his German shepherd soared over a short section of fence wound with fake greens. At the apex, his hind legs kicked back magnificently. Ears perked, eyes forward, the animal seemed every bit as joyous as any human athlete achieving a formidable goal.

"*So ist brave,*" the proud owner congratulated him.

"Good boy, good dog," Monk translated.

Across the field the woman put her shepherd in a down-stay then walked perhaps sixty yards without turning to look back. She used an oval hand mirror to keep her eye on the dog.

Downfield, another woman yelled, "She crawled a little bit, Polly," when the large, dark shepherd inched forward on its belly. Polly nodded and turned back.

A second man joined Monk and me. He was tall, perhaps six-two, and wore what was left of his white hair nearly shaved bald. His right thumb hung on the pocket of his jeans below a faded T-shirt that accentuated a small paunch. His left hand held some object out of sight behind his back. The stance was just short of intimidating, curious without being threatening–yet. Whatever he heard about me would either loosen those massive shoulders or tighten his whole body into a fist.

Monk performed the introductions. Glancing between the two men, I noticed Garry had wandered over to chat up another boy about his own size and a younger girl with long fair hair. The kids wore shorts and T-shirts and sneakers, like any American kids on any balmy summer evening.

"You a reporter?" the man named Bill asked without preamble. He wiped sweat from his forehead with his short sleeve.

I blinked with genuine surprise. "No," I assured him. "I'm a friend of Linda Arden," surely this was becoming truer by the minute, "and she asked me to see what can be done for Tibor. Since he's a schutzhund champion, I thought I ought to find out what that means."

Bill regarded me for a second and then grunted. "Well, if you're gonna stay awhile, you'll have to sign this." The object he'd been carrying was a clipboard with a stack of legally worded waivers on it. Basically, it meant the Delaware Valley Schutzhund Club didn't want to be held responsible for Garry's or my safety.

I glanced around. What I saw were about twenty people in the thirty to fiftyish age range, almost as many women as men, and five children. With them, awaiting their turns on the field, were several German shepherds, two rottweilers and a couple of smaller, shepherdlike dogs I later learned were malenois.

Needless to say, Garry and I were the only outsiders. The group projected a closeness that seemed to repel strangers, like a family bonded together by hard times. If I hadn't needed a handle on how to help Linda and Tibor, I would have handed the clipboard back and gone home. Instead, I accepted the offered ballpoint pen and signed the waiver with a flourish.

Bill nodded curtly and returned to his dog.

The three kinds of jumps had been removed and men were setting up six tall, red, triangular blinds in two widely spaced rows which encompassed almost the whole field. Made of cloth, the two-sided blinds looked like skinny teepees just wide enough to hide a man. The men placing them worked like brothers who had been schooled in their father's business since they were teens; their movements were that natural, that smooth.

To my left, another club member had just finished climbing into padded overalls. Now, he stuck his left arm into a plastic sleeve hinged at the elbow. The entire exterior of the sleeve was thickly padded with what looked like burlap or maybe woven rope. From his barrel of supplies the man then extracted a supple, thirty-inch padded stick with a loop for carrying it on his wrist. A little chill of concern electrified my limbs.

Just as I was wondering how in the world to ask my rather nervy, probing questions, Garry came up to Monk and me, bright-eyed and as ingenuous as only an eleven-year-old can be. "Why'd they fire the gun?" he asked Monk.

Gun? I hadn't even heard it.

Monk's eyes crinkled up with a paternal smile. "Part of their training, son," the sandy-haired man explained. "Protection dogs can't be afraid of guns. So, we fire a starter's pistol a couple times during their obedience trials. The dog's allowed to acknowledge the noise, but he's not supposed to let it distract him."

Garry's forehead wrinkled thoughtfully. "What're they doing now?" he asked.

Monk lowered himself into a restful crouch. "The object of the sport is to show off the breed's criteria. You have a dog?"

"An Irish setter," Garry admitted.

"Well, they're hunting dogs. They instinctively know how to sneak up on a bird, flush it out, and then retrieve it. Your dog do any of that?"

"Yeah," Garry agreed eagerly. "Gretsky loves fetching a tennis ball, and sometimes he stalks pigeons in the back yard. It's really funny to watch."

"Okay," Monk said. "Your dog stalks birds. Our dogs are bred to protect their owners."

I wondered how he might explain Tibor turning on Karl, but now wasn't the time to ask. A small commotion riveted our attention.

Off to our right the man in the padded overalls was slapping the ground with a short whip. A young German shepherd at the end of a fifteen-foot lead secured to a telephone pole snapped and barked at the padded man, but the man remained just out of his reach. Nearby, the dog's owner, a woman, congratulated the animal and urged him on. Finally, the man offered his padded arm for the dog to bite. The dog complied, but only for a brief moment. The owner warbled and cooed her approval.

Meanwhile, I was suppressing a major-league twitch. The nasty-sounding growling and barking had pushed some instinctive buttons inside me, and I wanted to yelp and run. By his pale face and wide eyes I could tell Garry was also frightened and a little shocked.

"So, the obedience phase is probably the most useful part of the sport, then the tracking part," Monk continued to explain from his crouch. "The biting part they're working on with the young dog over there is to show how courageous the animal can be.

"Now out in the field Larry is working on Drigon's Schutzhund Three—the same level work Tibor does." During the latter comment Monk stood and made a point of looking at me. I remained adamantly impassive, which Monk seemed to accept. He continued the lesson with a hand on Garry's shoulder.

"First the dog will search each blind–think of them as rooms in a house. If he finds an intruder, which he will when he gets to the last one there, the dog's supposed to contain him with barks and growls. If the intruder makes a move to escape, the dog's supposed to bite onto his arm and not let go. A good bite is one where you can't see any daylight between the teeth and the arm."

Heart pounding, I tried to breathe normally and not transfer my emotional response to either Garry or Monk. They didn't need to know I was imagining Tibor's canines sunk deep into his owner's throat.

After the shouted command, *"Boron,"* Drigon cautiously searched each blind until he came to the make-believe intruder. *"Passauf,"* he was instructed, or "Watch, hold at bay," and *"Gebault,"* which meant, "Speak."

When the padded man swung left as if to flee, Drigon attacked so swiftly I didn't have time to blink. The man tried to shake him off and failed. Then he swatted the dog's flank with the supple stick swinging from his free arm–once, twice.

"To show bravery," Monk informed us in a hushed voice.

Drigon held. The owner ordered, *"Aus,"* and the dog released the sleeve, eased back, and watched–eyes sparkling, tongue dripping. The pleased owner permitted him to carry the padded sleeve around for a while like a trophy.

I reminded myself to breathe. "Wow," I said. "That's amazing."

Garry remained exceptionally quiet. The other boy had wandered nearby, and my son gravitated toward him with only a quick glance to ask my permission.

"Would you say schutzhund dogs are well trained in the conventional sense?" I asked Monk. His attention had drifted off as he absently fondled his own German shepherd's ears. The animal was maybe eighty pounds, beautifully colored with a blond ruff and legs and less black fur than some shepherds. Her eyes were a golden brown, alert with intelligence.

Monk switched to rubbing his own chin while he considered my question. "Teaching commands other than the ones we use in schutzhund confuses the dog, so we don't discipline our dogs on an everyday basis like other trainers. But if you're thinking of Tibor, he was probably more domesticated than these others. Linda's influence. She kept Tibor inside like a pet. When Karl had him, Tibor slept outside like the rest of our dogs do."

"Could the differences in treatment have stressed Tibor out enough to make him attack Karl?"

"Naw," Monk replied. "Tibor's an exceptional dog. He could handle it. And he loved Karl. They were a real partnership. Couldn't have won his Schutzhund Three otherwise."

I nodded, but I wondered.

An owner walked by with her dog, the dog wearing something strapped to its head that I had first seen during the obedience practice. Because of the short antenna extending up beside the dog's ear, I thought the apparatus was a walkie-talkie for issuing commands at long distances. I asked about it.

"Walkie-talkie?" My instructor seemed very puzzled by my description. "Oh, no. It's a correctional device. Electrical." As in *electrical shock*. Monk widened his eyes to ask whether he needed to elaborate.

He didn't.

During Gretsky's fifth or sixth week with us, it had been necessary to install a pulsing electrical wire a foot inside the normal fencing around our back yard. Rip and I had debated long and hard about what we considered to be an extreme measure, but our spirited pup had been tunneling under or leaping over our ordinary four-foot fence about once or twice a day–and he never looked both ways before crossing a street.

As it turned out, we should have rented the device because Gretsky was cured of that particular bad habit in exactly one second. Now, not only does he stay inside the fence, he also avoids my fuzzy bedroom slippers for fear of getting zapped by static electricity.

Obviously, schutzhund enthusiasts took their sport quite seriously.

And yet it was only a sport.

Monk grimaced into the distance as if he had sensed my disapproval. He sighed and folded his arms to address me. "If you're putting pressure on a dog and the dog doesn't understand why, that's abuse," he explained. "But when the dog knows what's expected of him but he doesn't feel like doing it, the compulsion is a learning tool. He's learning how to take the pressure off himself."

I remained skeptical. Monk sighed again and shook his head. "These are guard dogs, Ms. Barnes. We train them with play as long as we can, but when they get a little older, they get ornery, like teenagers."

He had me there. I nodded once.

"You've been there," Monk observed. I nodded again with a dismissive shrug. "So you know. There comes a time when we have to use force to make them concentrate. Each dog has his own schedule, and we try to make sure each one is ready for the next step before we go ahead."

Monk's information unbalanced me, enough to morph me into a mental Switzerland–neutral but vigilant. Film now, edit later. This was a European short-subject after all and nothing a regular American woman should expect to absorb in an instant.

So it was with an uncommon detachment that I observed Garry sitting cross-legged in the shade with the other boy, deep in conversation. Farther away the two puppies gamboled in the grass.

And over on the field another dog was having a go-around with the padded man. This time the snarling and barking were merely noise, the owner's congratulations part of the dog's training, the circling with and shaking of the trophy sleeve symbolic of accomplishment.

"You ever get protesters?" I asked aloud.

Monk folded his arms across his sturdy chest. "Funny you should ask," he said. "Karl had a run-in with one a couple weeks ago. Real flake. Just stood right over there watching us with her wimpy boyfriend, but you could tell they were angry, not at all interested in our perspective." He eyed me with as much acceptance as I was likely to get, and I realized my effort to understand the sport before drawing any conclusions was the only reason Monk was still talking to me.

"Karl got here just as Bill was showing them the waiver, you know, thinking he could scare them off. But the woman took one look at Karl and flipped out. 'You,' she said, 'You're the diet doctor who makes people eat meat.' Then she started yelling that he was a killer and an animal abuser and plenty of nasty stuff you wouldn't think could come out of her mouth. She even tried to go after Karl with her fists, but Tibor came between them and growled. The young man pulled the woman back real fast, but she kept cursing all the way back to their car. Karl kept Tibor under control, but it could have been ugly."

"Who was she? Did anybody know her?"

Monk shook his head. "Naw. She was just some flake."

"What did she look like?"

"Just a little bit of a thing. So high. No meat on her. Pointy little nose. Short blond hair."

Great. A five-foot-tall, thin, blond vegetarian. These days there were probably a few females of that description on any page of any phone book.

"Too bad you didn't get her name," I lamented.

Monk rubbed his chin some more over my disappointment. Then he suddenly brightened. "She wore a Francisvale T-shirt." Birthday candles shined gaily in his eyes.

"What's Francisvale?" I wondered aloud.

"Francisvale Home for Smaller Animals? It's an animal shelter. She probably works there."

"Might help," I conceded.

The barking and growling were getting to me again. Also, I could see that Monk's turn with his dog was coming up.

"Just one more question," I said. "Could Tibor's

attack on Karl have been some sort of freak accident?"

Monk started shaking his head no before I completed the question. "No way," he told me emphatically. "You can see what these dogs are willing to do for us. You need a real strong partnership to make it work. Karl and Tibor were real close. Real close."

"So how do you explain what happened?"

Monk wagged his head slowly and tsked. "Only thing I can figure is somebody got to him."

"To Tibor?"

"Yeah. Somebody had to have trained him to do that. You know what I mean?"

He meant that Tibor's inducement to do Karl harm had to have been greater than his desire to protect him.

"Yes," I said. "I do know what you mean."

Unfortunately.

Chapter 7

ON THE RIDE home from the schutzhund practice Garry was so quiet I allowed him time to sort through his impressions.

Just as I was getting worried enough to prompt a conversation, he told me, "Petey said they're just dogs." Petey could only be the boy he met at the field.

Illuminating. While stating the obvious, Garry's observation also spoke volumes. To avoid diluting the poetry of it, I gave my son an approving glance.

The next morning I pretty much forgot about Tibor and Linda. Bryn Derwyn's camp was again short on counselors, so this time Rip took me up on my offer to help out.

From nine to eleven it was me and three rotating groups of youngsters clumped together by approximate age. Chelsea stayed with her six-year-olds, but I was assigned to Arts and Crafts.

What to do, what to do? Egg-carton tulips were out because you have to save cartons for months in advance. You also need pipe cleaners and children with absolutely no trace of imagination, which pretty much ruled out every kid I ever met.

Dodge ball? Kick ball? Old favorites from my remote youth. Sports were not my assignment.

Weaving things from gimp, the flat plastic string that comes in such inspiring colors? Highly impractical, because it necessitated a trip to a store fifteen miles away.

So it was pine-cone bird feeders or nothing.

This involved collecting pine cones from under the school's large trees behind the baseball field. With some additional time for running around in the woods, that took up at least fifteen minutes of the forty-five-minute periods. Much time was spent scooping peanut butter out of the five large jars (purchased at the grocery store for the purpose), pushing it into the pine cones, and licking fingers. Taking turns rolling the prickly globules in birdseed took five minutes, but attaching a piece of string seemed to take no time at all. We wrapped the finished products in waxed paper, labeled each one, and stored them in the campers' personal cubbyholes in the lower school hallway.

"Do these things work?" inquired a cherub in chartreuse shorts who obviously cut her own bangs.

"Certainly," I assured her. "The squirrels love them."

At eleven the whole batch of campers, all sixty-five of them, grabbed their swimsuits, towels, and lunches and clambered into the two buses waiting in the school's front circle. Rip had arranged for daily time at a nearby pool where the kids would take turns receiving swimming instruction or playing around. Afterward they would eat lunch in the surrounding park.

Nobody needed me for any of this, so I phoned Linda from Rip's office. "May I come over for a few minutes?" I asked.

"Why?" Linda responded.

Because I'm trying to help you, I wanted to shout, but her barricade was too thick.

I took a deep breath and reminded myself that people only denied what they were not ready to face. "Matter of national policy," I quipped instead.

"What?"

"Helping those who can't help themselves," *or won't,* I thought to myself.

"Really, Gin, I don't need…"

"Not you," I interrupted. "Tibor. You asked me to get Tibor back."

"Can you?" *Now* she got enthusiastic. Go figure.

"That's what I want to talk about. Do you have a few minutes? I've got to come back to camp after lunch."

"Sure."

By the time we were settled together on padded iron benches under Linda's grape arbor I was acutely aware that it was noon. My stomach craved something–anything–more solid than the iced tea it was being offered.

My hunger was probably why I asked about Karl's work first. "I know he was in demand as a weight-loss expert, but I don't know anything about his methods."

Linda reflected on this and looked over my shoulder toward the tennis court. She wore baggy denim-colored shorts with a white knit shirt tucked in tight enough to cause envy. My stomach grumbled just looking at her belt size.

"To hear Karl talk about it, his plan was highly scientific, but it was really pretty simple," she answered "You liked it, you couldn't have it."

"I don't understand."

"Whatever you craved, he told you to eat the opposite. Usually that meant starving on carrots and celery for a couple months, but occasionally he recommended large quantities of protein."

Meat, the substance of the protester's complaint.

"And exercise, of course," Linda added.

"Did it work?"

Karl's ex-wife shrugged. "That's a little more difficult to answer."

"Often enough," I suggested.

"Yes," she agreed. Often enough to establish Karl's reputation. Often enough for him to afford a large piece of land close to the city, nice clothes, nice car, women on the side, and so on.

"Were his diets healthy?" I asked.

Again, Linda shrugged. "Short term."

I nodded and sipped my tea. "Did you know that a protester–an animal rights activist–caused a ruckus at schutzhund practice a few weeks ago?"

"No."

"Small blond woman, short hair, pointy nose. Any idea who she was?"

"No. Where are you going with this, Gin?"

"Just trying to do what you asked," I said easily.

"It doesn't sound like it."

"If somebody else was responsible for Karl's death, the judge will probably release Tibor back to you," I explained. "The schutzhund people told me he wouldn't have turned on Karl without a pretty extreme incentive. Which means if you didn't retrain him, somebody else did."

Linda shook her head with disbelief. "That's preposterous. How?"

"I know you allowed Tibor to stay inside overnight, but Karl put him outdoors in a kennel. Was it locked?"

Linda merely glared, which I took as a negative answer. "So. Do you have any idea who hated Karl?"

"Other than me?" She made a dismissive "puh" sound and her eyes trailed off toward the driveway.

I wanted to shake her shoulders and tell it like it was. You've been arrested for murder. It will not go away unless you DO SOMETHING.

Over in the drive a man with the air of an employee had begun to wash her car. Linda's eyes glossed over him, then found their way back to me. She seemed to wonder why I was still there.

I had a momentary insight: In recent months, maybe even years, Linda hadn't been close enough to Karl to have any idea who else might have hated him.

"Okay," I conceded. "Who should I ask?"

Linda blinked as she watched the dark man in khaki sponge dirt off her Lincoln. "Akeesha, I guess."

"And she is?"

"Karl's office manager."

Now I remembered. She discovered Karl's body. Maybe she would still be around closing up the office in his house.

Linda bit her lip and frowned at the grapevine shadows as if she suspected something loomed just above, something she could not quite see.

I wondered. Was this repression of hers just ordinary cowardice? Extraordinary cowardice? Was I insensitive to wish she would just plain buck up?

I once heard of a thoroughbred named "Oh, Don't Worry" who hated to race. She dealt with her problem by running like crazy for the finish line. That was me, the practical horse. But even the ones who, like Linda, shied away from the starting gate could be schooled...

"Talked to your dad lately?" I asked.

The accused's casual countenance snapped shut like a mousetrap, so I rose to go.

Linda also stood with a sigh and began to escort me around the side of the house.

I took a chance and mentioned that Tibor only had eight days of quarantine left.

Linda drew in another deep breath. "I appreciate what you're trying to do," she said with apparent difficulty. "It's just..." Her fingers made a little waving gesture to signify confusion.

"Do you want me to continue?"

Linda looked directly at me, and for the first time I felt she knew perfectly well I was helping her as much as, or more than, her dog. The woman's self-esteem was simply so low that she found it almost impossible to acknowledge her own needs.

"Do you want to?" she asked.

"Yes," I replied.

Linda nodded, and tears welled up in her dark eyes.

"You've forgotten about food again," I reminded her.

She laughed, but I didn't. I had really wanted her to offer me lunch.

Chapter 8

I STOPPED AT home to fix myself a no-fat cream cheese and apple butter sandwich on whole wheat, skim milk on the side. The bulk quieted the squawking baby birds who'd taken up residence in my gut, and the no-fat/skim part salved my conscience. I wasn't exactly overweight, but I wasn't perfectly satisfied with my shape either. Me and ninety-nine percent of the rest of the population.

After lunch, I offered Gretsky a romp in the yard. He ran after my toss exactly once then feinted left as I tried to grab back the tennis ball. Game over. My punishment for tricking Davy Crockett.

"Want to go for a ride in the car?" I suggested in an effort to repair my reputation.

Oh, boy, do I? said Gretsky's dash past my knees. I didn't have to bother clipping on a leash, although I brought it along for later.

As soon as I steered my relatively new Subaru wagon into Bryn Derwyn's drive, I could see softball and Wiffle-Ball baseball were being played left and right by almost everyone in camp. Only the medically exempt seemed to be keeping score or retrieving bats.

When I stopped in the front circle, Rip emerged from the front door of the sprawling brick school and stuck his head in the passenger window to rub Gretsky's ears.

"You're off the hook this afternoon," he told me, "but you don't have to look so cheery about it." Apparently, the news had brightened my face.

"Sorry," I apologized. Although I probably could have maintained my maternal patience for another few hours, I was eager to finish my commitment to Linda and her father.

Gretsky quivered beneath Rip's hand, evidently

hoping to get his lips around a Wifflle-Ball, maybe prompt a good keep-away game with a bunch of campers.

My husband smiled tolerantly at him. "Not this time, buddy," he said. "You've got to keep my wife out of trouble, you hear?"

"Oh, go play with your Legos and don't worry about me," I replied, wiggling my fingers to indicate the four cement-block walls rising from a rectangular ditch to the right of the school.

In no way did the gym's cheap-looking foundation appear worth the cost and aggravation I knew the project had engendered. Easy to understand why a school administration usually procrastinates as long as possible before assuming such a commitment. Since Rip felt he'd been saddled with this particular responsibility prematurely, the relief of finally having it financed and under way was major. In fact, his eyes twinkled at the very mention of it. We exchanged warm smiles and a very brief kiss. After all, children were watching, ours included.

I tried not to burn rubber distancing myself from all those energetic little bodies. Akeesha would either be at Karl's former office or she wouldn't.

He was.

Two cars graced the lengthy drive of Karl's Chestnut Hill property, a small green compact and the same rust-corroded station wagon I had seen at Linda's less than two hours before.

To my surprise, the Hispanic man who had washed Linda's car was now occupied hosing out a kennel set a short distance from Karl's garage. Apparently the handyman's hours had also been divvied up in the divorce.

"Hi," I called to him as I approached. "Could I ask you a favor?"

The man was about six feet tall, pock-marked by

some previous scarring skin condition, and stoop-shouldered in thw subservient way some men wear like a disguise. A black moustache curved straight down from his upper lip to his chin, and he wore a lightweight straw hat to shield his receding hairline from the early afternoon sun. I learned about the hairline when he tipped the hat toward me.

He waited to hear the favor before saying one word, and I began to worry whether he understood English.

"My dog is with me and it's getting pretty hot out," I began. "May I use the kennel while I go inside for a few minutes?" The rear of the chain-link run was sheltered by a long, shady roof.

"Of course," said the man. Yet his words were spoken with the lilt and warmth of the Spanish language.

I thanked him and went back for Gretsky.

When I returned, only a freshly filled water bowl remained inside the enclosure. A lawnmower chugged into life nearby.

I took note of the latch on the dog-run gate: a typical forked metal enclosure–dog-proof, but no challenge to a human over the age of two.

Gretsky gave me a questioning glance as I ushered him into his temporary accommodations, so I fondled his chin and assured him I wouldn't be long. He waited for me to walk three steps away before beginning to bark.

I ignored him and proceeded toward Karl's house, another gray stone edifice complete with moss and a crusty slate roof. Perhaps when Linda and he had been a couple, she encouraged him to purchase a place that looked like home to her.

Or maybe they simply lusted for the land. Very few properties this close to the city could boast of so much space, ten acres at least. Both distance and overgrown trees and shrubs insured peace and quiet any time of day or night. Except for the occasional horn or siren, the nearby city traffic sounded quite a bit like ocean surf. The flat front yard resembled a park, but possessed enough open area for any sized obedience class Linda could put together.

I was curious about the spot where Karl had been killed. The newspapers had described it as a small, secluded field beyond the thicket of trees behind the house. Regardless, teams of forensic folks and reporters had probably trampled it clueless.

Hanging from a curved wrought-iron post, a discreet black sign with white lettering directed me toward Karl's office where an old black screen door led into what may have been a kitchen earlier in the century. With a couple stone walls between me and the kennel, Gretsky's voice became chalk across somebody else's blackboard.

Inside, a woman leaned over a file drawer with her back toward me. My view was of matching brown elbows, a dark green tank top, and a flat trim backside sheathed in white slacks.

"Akeesha?" I asked from the doorway.

The woman whirled around and held her fist to her heart. She also made a scared little yip. Barely discernible eyebrows arched with dismay.

"Who are you?" Karl's former office manager asked more from surprise than poor manners.

"Gin Barnes, a friend of Linda Arden's. Do you have a minute?"

She tossed the long black braids that had landed on her shoulder back where they belonged and prompted a touch of jealousy. My own nutmeg-colored mop refused to do anything more than cap my head like an acorn lid.

Recovering herself, the young woman, for she appeared to be little more than twenty, offered me a seat on one of the oversized green leather captain's chairs in front of the reception desk. Back to the left a walnut door appeared to lead to Karl's inner office. All around us were shelves of books interspersed with dog trophies. The largest was a tarnished silver bowl mounted on a wooden base. Inside were a couple of golf tees, a twist tie, and some paper clips.

All in all, it was an oppressively academic, blatantly masculine room–in my opinion. I couldn't imagine enduring the unrelieved weightiness of it eight hours a day.

And then I remembered Karl's specialty was weight loss. That, at least, explained the stalwart chairs. Thinking of all the desperately unhappy people who exposed their frailties inside these rooms made me feel as if those thick heavy chairs had been stacked on my shoulders.

"Sure," Akeesha agreed. "I could use a break. You want a Coke?" The temperature in the room was probably eighty with only a small metal electric fan to stir things around.

"That'd be great." Diet Coke, of course. From a can. Either Akeesha had always had kitchen privileges or discovering her boss's body had eliminated any worry about pillaging his refrigerator.

"Can we sit outside?" I asked with a wince.

"Yeah, me, too," the business manager agreed, fanning herself with a graceful hand. "We'll go over by that bush." She led the way out to a curved stone bench beside an eight-foot tall boxwood. Its sweet fragrance combined with the smell of damp loam and sun-warmed stone.

Akeesha straddled the sunny end of the bench. I cooled the bottom of my cotton walking shorts on the shady end.

"What can I do for you?" she asked.

"First, maybe I should ask what you think happened

out there." I gestured toward the back of the house.

Akeesha's face dropped, and she actually shivered in the late June heat. "I honestly don't know. It was awful–I can tell you that."

"Do you think it was an accident?"

"I don't know much about dogs."

"You think the police have a case against Dr. Vogel's ex-wife?"

"You're her friend. Do you?"

I shook my head and set down my Coke can. "No," I answered automatically. Then I reconsidered the question–it's good to scan the data banks now and again–but the answer came up the same. "No," I repeated.

"So, what do you want from me?"

"I started out trying to get Tibor back for Linda, but I quickly realized it's all the same package. Linda's in big trouble unless somebody comes up with an alternate explanation to the one the police concocted.

"I've watched her handle Tibor, and I can't imagine her mistreating him the way he had to have been mistreated to make him turn on Karl. Since Linda wasn't much help coming up with other suspects, I'm wondering whether you know anybody else who hated Karl enough to go to such an extreme."

Akeesha huffed out a little laugh. Naturally, she would be quite familiar with the details of the Vogels' divorce. "It all seems so far-fetched."

Yet even as she made the remark, she seemed to be remembering the manner of Karl's death. "Oh, boy," she sighed. "You want the names of dissatisfied clients, don't you?"

"Just the really hostile ones."

Akeesha widened those beautiful black eyes. "Okay," she sighed. "Debbie Greene's father comes to mind first, Colin Greene."

I prompted her for a bit more detail.

Karl's office manager shook her head sadly. "Debbie died of anorexia nervosa; in other words, she starved herself to death. The father blamed Dr. Vogel, but it really wasn't his fault. I don't think anybody could have reached Debbie."

"How long ago was this?"

"Two years, but Colin Greene still blames Dr. Vogel. He called up drunk just last month and gave him quite an earful. I was across the room and I could hear Mr. Greene shouting through the phone."

"Did he do that often?"

"Now and then."

"Anybody else?"

Akeesha thought a minute. "Annie' Snellenberg, I guess."

This time I encouraged her with an expectant expression.

"Failed dieter," she elaborated.

"That's enough?"

"She seems to think so. Lots of unresolved issues there. Angry, unresolved issues."

I nodded, figuring I would find out more by talking to Annie herself.

"Anyone else?"

Akeesha pursed her lips and thought for a minute. "Darlene Polk maybe. And Nancy Carlino for sure."

"Who are they?"

"Darlene's another dissatisfied customer. Nancy's my predecessor." The way she smiled when she said that especially intrigued me.

"Karl fired her—she claims because she became overweight. Really it was because she started discouraging clients from undergoing treatment. Told whoever would listen they shouldn't be so hung up about their size, that she was fat and didn't mind one bit."

"Bad for business," I suggested.

"Quite."

"But not a reason to kill anybody."

"Oh, I don't know. Nancy filed a discrimination lawsuit that promised to make her rich and her lawyer famous."

"At Karl's expense though." I wiggled my fanny on the hard stone bench. "Didn't that give Karl more of a motive to eliminate Nancy?"

Akeesha shook her head slowly. "Her case hasn't looked too good lately."

"Oh," I said, seeing her point. "Disappointing."

"Quite."

"Anybody else?" I asked.

"Isn't that enough?"

I assured her it was probably enough to put a whole homicide unit on a regimen of Tums. Unless, of course, they were still satisfied with their initial arrest.

"And now, if you'll be kind enough to tell me where to find these people, I'd better check on my dog. He's not barking."

"Isn't that good?" Akeesha asked.

"Not necessarily."

When I finally approached the kennel, Gretsky treated me to a sloppy grin. Held between his paws was the largest soup bone I'd ever seen, possibly part of an ox. Separating him from it was more of a risk than I chose to undertake. The question was: How was I going to transport a greasy dog and his smelly, greasy bone without ruining the upholstery of my car?

The kennel/yard man must have been anticipating the problem. He appeared as if by magic, opened the gate, hauled Gretsky out by the scruff of his neck, and clipped on the leash I had left draped over the fence. With his thick leather shoe, he kicked the bone out of range.

Gretsky blinked up at the man as if anticipating lightning bolts. Growling or snapping hadn't even occurred to him; and I realized if he hadn't responded aggressively with a large bone at stake, he probably never would. I felt as if Karl and Linda's employee had just given me a delicate vase made of very thin glass.

"Thanks," I told the man, "for everything."

He tipped his hat for sure that time and headed back to his lawnmower.

I stooped down to rub Gretsky's ears face-to-face. "Good, good boy," I said. "Maybe we should rename you Gandhi."

Our pacifist Irish setter warmed to my tone, if not my meaning, and delivered a smelly dog kiss up the side of my cheek.

As we shambled slowly back to my car, Gretsky only glanced back toward the bone three or four times.

Chapter 9

WHILE GRETSKY and I sat in Karl's drive waiting for the Subaru's air conditioning to do something, I splurged and asked Information for Francisvale's number on my cell phone. Then I actually placed the call.

"This is going to sound a little strange," I admitted to the person who answered. "But I need to talk to a woman who was wearing one of your T-shirts."

"What's her name?" the female voice asked reasonably.

I don't know, but she's about five feet tall, thin, and has short blond hair. Oh, and I think she's a vegetarian." The "pointy nose" description could be a last resort.

"Oh, you must mean Stevie Luckenbill. Hold on. I'll get her."

"She's there?"

"Sure. She volunteers all the time, but let me get her. She's about ready to leave."

"Wait!" I shouted into the cellular phone. "I'm in my car. Please ask her to wait until I get there. It's important." I held the woman on the line long enough to get directions to the Francisvale Home for Smaller Animals, which happened to be on a hillside at the corner of Upper Gulph and Arden roads, a coincidence merely and no relation to Linda's last name. (I specifically asked at one point.) The mailing address was Radnor, the phone exchange Bryn Mawr, and the actual location probably Gulph Mills–a prime example of the Main Line's sleights-of-hand designed to irritate and confuse non-natives.

Four cars already vied for space in a gravel lot that was scarcely a dent in the fencing. To my surprise, inside the tall chain-link enclosure were lots of little tombstones among the grass and shrubbery, for Francisvale was as much a pet cemetery as it was an animal shelter.

Luckily, the trees made the area ten degrees cooler than at Kurt Vogel's, so I felt able to leave Gretsky in the car with the windows open. At last glance he was sprawled on the back bench wiggling his nose in the air and looking contemplative.

Letting myself onto the property through a couple of gates, I made my way uphill to a bush-enclosed, squat building that appeared to be the main place of business. Farther uphill sat a residence and, off to its right, what appeared to be kennels with generous outdoor runs. Penned inside were a number of medium-sized dogs of indeterminate breed. Each seemed equally glad to see me, although they all voiced it in their own way.

I stuck my head inside the screened door of the main building before I insinuated my whole self into the crowded room. There was no reception desk, no buffer whatsoever from the operations part. In fact a fluffy old golden retriever seemed to be receiving a much-needed sponge bath just inside the door.

A small workroom with a sink, bathtub, and a couple of cages lay to the right. Cat cages lined the wall opposite me and continued around a doorway on the left. Everywhere supplies were stored in strict, apple-pie order, which still managed to look ragged because of the close quarters and apparent wear. Also, there was a smell–part disinfectant, part wet golden retriever, part unknown.

The fluffy-haired woman on the floor glanced up at me without allowing the wet dog to squirm away. I noticed several stitches closing a wound on the animal's side.

"I'm looking for Stevie Luckenbill," I said hopefully. "Is she still here?"

"Oh, yes," the woman answered. "Just around the

corner."

I made my way past the cages into the next room. Hung prominently on the wall was a yellow cat placemat that read, "He who dislikes the cat was in his former life a rat!"

Down at ground level an intensely helpful woman of Stevie's description transferred three caramel-and-white kittens into a carrier held by a brunette wearing a "Pals for Life" sweatshirt.

"You're adopting them?" I asked the eager recipient.

"No, but somebody might. I take them to nursing homes as pet therapy for the residents. It's a win-win proposition."

"Sounds good to me," I agreed.

Then as tactfully as all get-out, I asked whether the Francisvale volunteer was indeed Stevie Luckenbill–not much of a question because nobody else was in the room, just piles of towels, rugs, shelves of pet food, a washer and dryer, a bunch of stuffed toy animals, several caged cats, and one large crate of multicolored puppies.

"I'll come back for them," the brunette said, referring to the puppies.

"Good luck," said Stevie Luckenbill. "Now, what can I do for you, ma'am?"

Ma'am, as in madam? Me? Was this kid Southern or just terminally polite?

I hedged, not because I was unprepared, but because you don't just blurt out that somebody was a murder suspect–or if they weren't yet, soon could be.

"Can we go outside and talk?" I requested. "This is about Karl Vogel."

"Ugh. What a creep!" Stevie seemed to have no interest in maintaining privacy; but I was still in the doorway, and I sensed an increased interest from the woman working on the golden retriever.

"Please?" I asked.

"Oh, sure. I don't have any secrets from Maggie, but if you want to go outside, we can. I'll probably just keep goin', Mag," she announced as she passed by the other worker. "See you tomorrow?"

"No, I'm off."

"Monday then."

That was about the time I lost control of the conversation–before it started.

"Let's go over to the old part," Stevie suggested.

"Sure," I agreed. Why not? I thought. But then I would soon learn all of Stevie's suggestions turned out to be like that–reasonable but not necessarily what you wanted to do.

Once outside we turned our backs on the final resting places of Peanuts and Thomasina, Mr. Reds, the "unique" Rusty (1958-1974), Skippy and Mopsie, Feld Putzski "Our love 1970-1985" and the succession of Jones pets–Angel, Teddy, Judy, Twink, Marco, Duffy, and Sugar (all deceased). We ignored, or tried to ignore, Ratchet, who was "Gone Too Soon," and Dimidio Blackie, who had true grit and was well loved from 1970 to 1986 and probably beyond.

Stevie more or less bounced down the walk with tiny toes aimed outward. I couldn't actually see her toes, housed as they were inside tennis shoes; but the tennis shoes were impossibly tiny. Childlike even, and I began to feel inflated, like something you take to the beach to kick around.

Despite the heat, the young woman also wore tapered jeans and a surprise/surprise Francisvale Home for Smaller Animals T-shirt. The garment looked as laundered and overused as one of the towels back there on the shelf, but Stevie Luckenbill was so delicate I very quickly became more aware of her than her clothes.

The delicate impression ended at the gate into the old cemetery. Stevie Luckenbill turned to confront me.

"Now, what's this all about?" she asked. My cheeks felt scalded by her eyes. My hands began to sweat. This girl was easily ten years younger than me and probably twenty-five pounds lighter. Never mind. She had the candlepower of a laser.

I instantly dismissed my friend-of-Linda-Arden plan, going with, "I'm trying to save a dog named Tibor," instead.

"Go on …" Stevie's voice was high pitched but throaty, as if she had practiced cheerleading a little too long yesterday. She folded her fragile-looking arms across the "Home for Smaller" part of the T-shirt and affixed her blue eyes to the bridge of my nose.

As Monk described, her nose was indeed rather pointy; but it went with her narrow face and pixie ears, which were peeking out from underneath two feathery flaps of sun-streaked, honey-colored hair. There were furrows on her brow, premature by perhaps twenty or thirty years. Not from sun damage, I surmised, purely from concentrating on things–beginning with her crib mobile and continuing up to the bridge of my nose.

She wasn't exactly cute or pretty, but I felt compelled to look at her just the same. Maternal instinct, I suspected. This one had probably crawled up the stairs before she could walk, or maybe turned her mother gray by going through all the motions involved in starting a car–including releasing the hand brake, turning the ignition, and shifting into gear.

"First tell me something about Francisvale," I stalled. "I never heard of it before yesterday. What's the deal?" The brow creased a little deeper–with impatience, I suspected. "It's not named after St. Francis of Assisi, if that's what you think. Harriet Hare McClellan founded it and named it after her dog Francis, who came to her one snowy night. She gave us fifteen acres, only five of which are being used. We're solvent, but we're always glad for donations. We get an average of three calls a week for burial plots, and you saw the cats and dogs we shelter. They're all up for adoption."

"Do they usually get adopted?"

"Not as fast as we'd like."

"Has anybody suggested you might be a suspect in Karl Vogel's murder?" I asked abruptly.

"Murder?" She seemed genuinely shocked. "I thought his dog killed him."

"Somebody retrained the dog to do it. Could have been anybody. Some people are wondering whether it was you."

Stevie Luckenbill folded to the ground. Just like that. Her legs were holding her one minute and the next they were down, knees splayed Indian fashion, either Indian you liked best. The position looked very yoga to me, probably because her back remained so erect.

I joined her on the grass. She seemed to be staring at the tombstone of Inky Fetterolf (1939-1955). I was glad she was no longer trying to penetrate my skull.

"Why would anybody think that?" the young woman asked, with tears pooling in her blue eyes.

Since she seemed to expect an answer, I said, "Because you yelled at him in public and almost tried to punch him."

Fearing grass stains, I tried not to squirm too much on the cool, damp ground. And, believe me, watching Stevie Luckenbill's face dissolve made me want to squirm.

"I'm a pacifist," she said, as if the word explained everything about her. "I don't eat meat or wear leather or even kill bugs. How could anybody think I could teach a dog to attack its owner? It would be against everything I believe."

I might have said a shocking number of people were hypocrites, but Stevie had received enough shocks from me already.

"How'd you happen to pick up on Karl Vogel?" I asked, partly to diffuse the stare she was cranking up again.

She wagged her head and plucked at the grass in front of her ankles. "My boyfriend, Michael. He's…" her eyes lifted and went all dreamy, "…so dedicated. He came across a magazine article about schutzhund and we asked around. Turned out there was a bunch of people practicing it right under our noses, so we went over to see for ourselves."

"But you singled out Dr. Vogel–why?"

The young woman sniffed and wiped her eyes on the shoulder of her T-shirt. "Somebody at my food-for-life group mentioned he sometimes prescribed a meat diet. I looked him up in the library. He's just–was just–a nutritionist. Did you know that? He wasn't even a doctor."

I nodded. Although Karl's assumed title had been more descriptive than real, most people were content to overlook the affectation now that the man was dead. Stevie Luckenbill's quibbling over it further revealed her animosity.

"So when I recognized him at the schutzhund practice, it all came together for me–the ignorance of it all, the arrogance. I lost my temper. Michael's always telling me I need more patience. He's right, I guess."

Before she could get all dreamy about Michael again, I asked what she did with herself when she wasn't volunteering at Francisvale. If she had said she attended high school, I wouldn't have blinked; so it came as a surprise when she told me she was saving for college.

"Except I'm in between jobs right now. I used to

watch twin boys, but the family's away for the summer. Then the kids will start school."

"What about your family?"

She shook her head. "It's just Michael and me."

The modern way. When you don't have any relatives, you get to pick your own.

We stood up then, and I made a show of being interested in the tombstones. The best was for Nympsee and another Francis, a dog and horse respectively. Apparently, they had delivered newspapers together during the Depression.

As we began to head back toward the gate, Stevie paused to ask my opinion. Or maybe it was just an incredulous remark.

"Do you really think the police will suspect me?"

I shook my head as I replied, "Not after they meet you." She smiled then, and that made all the difference. She *was* cute and, if not pretty, eminently loveable.

Which was probably why I did what I did next. I took out my pen and my grocery list and asked for her phone number. "In case I hear of any job openings."

Of course, I already had the temporary camp job in mind, but I knew enough to ask Rip before mentioning it to Stevie. There could be any number of reasons why he might not want to hire her.

Was it my fault I couldn't guess what they were?

Chapter 10

MAKING A DOG do what you think he should is like an American insisting on shaking hands with a Chinese. Canines have had their own customs for centuries, and they're not particularly interested in adopting ours. Why is it so easy to forget that?

Gretsky scarcely hit the ground before he squirted his personal "Kilroy Was Here" on the nearest clump of grass poking through Francisvale's parking-lot fence. Up the hill the kenneled ones sent up a chorus of welcome but settled down as soon as Gretsky jumped back into the car.

"Happy now?" I asked irritably.

Apparently, he was.

I didn't drive off right away. Once again, I dug out my cell phone to call Linda's lawyer, Timothy Bedoes.

"How are you doing?" he asked way too eagerly.

I was afraid I'd get a bill if I wasted his time, so I answered with one word: "Fine."

"What have you found out?"

"Oh, some interesting stuff, and that's the reason I called."

"You're on your cell?"

"Yes..."

"Say no more." He paused as if to check his watch. "Can you come right over? I'll step out of my next appointment for a few minutes."

It would be easier to dump the whole matter back in his lap in person, so I agreed.

He gave me the address, which I poked into my elderly GPS. It turned out to be inside a tasteful building I'd never noticed tucked behind a bank I'd never noticed on Lancaster Avenue in Wayne. Thank goodness the temperature remained cool enough to let Gretsky sleep in the car. Tied to a tree, the whole neighborhood would have been treated to his barking.

The law firm's Ivy League decor made *me* want to snooze, but the air- conditioning quashed that notion. Although it was already late June, the receptionist wore long sleeves.

Her unguarded smile said she was glad to see me even if she didn't know why. Clients did not present themselves in cropped pants, T-shirts and Keds. Perhaps she thought I was there for directions, or to meet my spouse, or to sell Girl Scout cookies.

"Timothy Bedoes asked me to stop in," I explained. "I'm Ginger Barnes." Working undercover.

"Oh, yes. Right this way." The woman led me to a large conference room. It was empty except for an enormous oval table and about fifteen chairs. Before she left me alone, she assured me Mr. Bedoes would be right along.

Although that sounded too good to be true, it wasn't. Linda's attorney rushed in not a minute later, which informed me I was much more essential to Timothy Bedoes than I had any desire to be.

"So," he said. "What can you tell me?" He grasped both my hands with both of his. His were a little damp.

"I still have reservations about what I'm doing for Linda," I opened. "Wouldn't a professional investigator do a much better job?"

"Why don't you tell me what you've found out? Then we'll decide."

"Okay." I still had reservations but allowed him to gesture me into one of the mahogany chairs.

Bedoes put a foot on the next one and leaned on his thigh. His socks matched his light gray slacks, and his black slip-ons came with tassels. Nifty.

I related what Monk told me about Tibor needing a

strong incentive to turn on Karl, and how anyone could have taken the dog from his kennel to retrain him because the kennel wasn't kept locked.

"Wouldn't Tibor have barked at a stranger?"

"My dog certainly would have. But if this person knew enough about training, he or she would also have known how to keep Tibor quiet."

"Okay, we'll come back to that. What else?"

I ran through the list of suspects Akeesha had given me, and each of their motives–Debbie Greene's father, the disgruntled clients Annie Snellenberg and Darlene Polk. I mentioned Nancy Carlino's discrimination lawsuit, which really sparked the attorney's interest. Then I described my meeting with Stevie Luckenbill.

Bedoes grinned broadly when I finished. "Great stuff. Good work." Add another row of stars to my chart.

"So how about turning it over to a professional?" I suggested. Please?

Bedoes shook his head, and his face became thoughtful in a manipulative sort of way. "No. I think Judge Arden was right. We can't pay a pro enough to care like you do. Plus I don't think a private detective would have your sort of luck. We mostly hire them to track down witnesses, make sure they get to court–that sort of thing. No, I think what Linda needs is exactly what you're doing–checking into things discreetly, reporting back…"

"Don't most cases rely more on forensic evidence?" Facts? Proof?

"Yes. And the police are very good at gathering that. But sometimes they need to know where to look before they can find it."

The young attorney raked a hand through his thinning blond hair. "The thing is, we don't know whether the evidence will be good or bad for Linda. That's why your discretion is so important."

"I'm not wearing a disguise or hiding behind any drapes to get it."

"No, but you're not wearing a uniform either." He gave my pants and T-shirt a look-at-yourself gesture, which afforded me another of my insights, the kind you get when you realize you've been incredibly stupid.

To wit: If I turned up anything detrimental to Linda's case, I could be written off as a well-meaning but bumbling friend. If I turned up anything useful, a pro could quickly step in and take the credit.

"I'd like to quit," I said.

Bedoes bit his lip with those widely gapped teeth and wagged his head. "A jury's really going to hate the idea of a woman training a man's dog to kill him," he lamented. "Linda could get the max."

I remained silent.

"I know you've done this before—more than once."

"Twice," I said. Twice I would admit to. I still kept most of my first investigation to myself, largely to protect my husband's feelings.

Bedoes stood up and stretched his back. "Well, this time the police aren't even trying." He eased himself into the chair at my knee and dangled his hands over the front edge. "Your leads are great," he told me. "Why not see them through? If you find out they're dead ends, you're off the hook. In the meantime, we'll pursue the evidence route."

His expression went all sincere. "Judge Arden is counting on you, you know...and so is Linda."

I had to admit producing hors d'oeuvres for seventy guests six or seven times a year did not exactly validate my existence. Not to me anyway, and mine was the deciding vote.

Honesty also forced me to admit that the lucky times

I'd helped solve a crime had been more satisfying than anything I'd ever done short of giving birth. Unlike my husband's job, nothing in my everyday life made much of a tangible difference. Like most people, I had to make good use of my opportunities–not unlike my mother, the well- meaning, daft, and eminently irritating Cynthia Struve.

"Oh, all right," I told Bedoes. "But when we need a pro, we get a pro."

"Deal."

For a minute my mind drifted off, and Linda's attorney patiently watched me think. Then I clicked my cheek and shook my head.

"Too bad it wasn't some other dog that killed Karl," I said. Any other dog and the problem was solved.

"What?" the lawyer said. "What did you say?"

I snapped back from my mental side-trip. "I said it's too bad some other dog didn't kill Karl. It would be a lot easier to get Linda off."

"I like it. I really like it." Bedoes was up and spinning around. "Wow. The judge was right. You really are a gem."

I recognized that to be third-hand Cynthia talk, so I ignored it. But then Bedoes spun some more and rubbed his hands.

"Dianne! Dianne, come in here," he called through the doorway.

The elegant, efficient Dianne trotted in wearing an expression of concern.

"Get Dr. Fleming in Colorado," Bedoes said as he checked his watch. "You can do it now, it's late enough."

After Dianne departed to make the call, Bedoes treated me to more hand-rubbing and a gap-toothed grin.

"What's going on?" I asked. This bubbly, school-boy stuff made me itch.

"Don't you see? No, obviously not. We're going to bring in an expert for the autopsy–Dr. Mathias Fleming. He's a retired forensic pathologist, and I know he has experience with dog bites. Oh, why didn't I think of this before? If Fleming can give us a little reasonable doubt... even if he can't, he'll give us time. Oh, this is great. Great!"

"If you say so."

Bedoes looked as if he might kiss me, so I hastily rose to leave.

EVER SINCE we started Gretsky in Linda's Thursday-night Beginners' Class, my best friend Didi had been coming over to dinner, then accompanying us to class. With her she brought her new companion, Chivas Beagle, who was purchased mainly so Didi and I could have another childhood experience together. As we got older, Didi became more creative in that respect.

Needless to say, she was in between men at the time of the purchase.

Tonight, she burst in the door with "Chevy" (I spell that phonetically), off her lead and free to roam wherever she might. The young pup immediately turned her white toes toward my kitchen and the handful of kibble remaining in Gretsky's bowl. With Gretsky watching helplessly from two feet away, the kibble disappeared.

Our twelve-pound, four-legged guest then gave Gretsky an in-your-face poke in the nose, walked under him right front to left rear, circled his rump and went under him right rear to left front, then began bouncing along into the living room looking for a place to pee.

"Didi!" I called, but she was back at the front door effusing over my children, "Studley" and "Madame President."

Simultaneously scooping young Chivas Beagle up with my right hand and opening our sliding screen door, I tossed the multicolored pooch smoothly onto our patio. She was squatting and puddling before I finished standing upright. The expression on her brown and black baby face seemed to say, "Oh, well. Anywhere will do."

"When are you going to housebreak this dog?" I asked Chevy's owner, who now stood in the archway to the living room fingering the texture of a braided leather leash.

"She is housebroken. What do you mean?"

Didi, an unconsciously graceful blonde, currently owned the Beverage Barn, a beer distributorship on a highway outside of Ludwig. She once taught ballet, another time sold perfume in a department store. Recently she had insinuated herself into the office of a potential murderer in the interest of helping me. She was as predictable as a hurricane and sometimes just as welcome–just ask her mild-mannered ex-husband. After experiencing Didi, he took himself and his two daughters to Albuquerque to rest up. To my knowledge they have not yet returned.

"Help me set the table," I suggested to my lifelong friend while letting her companion back inside. Our two dogs ran around us toward the hall, Gretsky's nose low and close to Chevy's pointy black tail.

"Who's our instructor going to be?" my friend asked as she entered the kitchen and grabbed a handful of everyday flatware from a drawer.

We had been through Linda's arrest and my peripheral involvement over the phone. Didi took it all in stride, but then she never raises a perfectly penciled eyebrow over anything I do.

"Roxanne," I answered. Linda had wisely decided against conducting the classes herself. Accused murderers have, after all, been accused of murder.

"Ugh. Isn't she that ditzy blonde?"

"No. You're the ditzy blonde. Roxanne is the chubby girl with the unfortunate lisp whose hair happens to be...blond."

"I stand corrected. You're not having eggplant tonight, are you?"

"Once," I shouted. "I gave you fried eggplant once, and you've mentioned it fifty times now. Give it up already."

"Well, are you?"

"No."

"So, what are we having?"

"Leftover ham and corn fritters."

"Well, that's all right then. Molasses or corn syrup?"

"Mrs. Butterworth's Lite, *if* it's all right with you."

Corn syrup would be nice."

I raised a frying pan over her head.

"Mrs. Butterworth's is good."

I lowered the pan.

"Any ice cream for dessert?"

I raised the pan.

"Girls, girls," Rip intervened as he leaned casually against the doorjamb.

"Oh, hi," I told him. "Got something for you." I handed him Stevie Luckenbill's phone number, and as I would eventually realize, also my grocery list. "A prospect for the temporary camp job. She's good with kids and animals–and she happens to be vegetarian," I added for the benefit of my finicky guest.

"Where'd you meet this girl?" Rip pressed before Didi and I could go off on another tangent.

"She volunteers at Francisvale Home for Smaller Animals."

Didi snorted. "The day pigs and cows can sit down

and discuss whether or not I should eat meat is the day I'll listen."

I opened my mouth to reply, but Rip beat me to it. "You really think this girl might be okay with the campers?"

"More-than okay. I think they'd love her. And she's available."

Rip stuck Stevie's number (and my grocery list) into his breast pocket and told me he'd phone her in the morning.

Didi and I stopped for ice cream cones on the way to Beginners' Class. I managed to prevent Gretsky from washing my face afterward. I'm not positive, but I think Didi gave Chevy the last half of her cone.

I parked the Subaru wagon next to the other cars on the grass at the side of Linda's drive. A few other class members were surreptitiously trying to catch sight of her through the windows, but her Lincoln wasn't in the garage, so I doubted she was home.

Gradually the assortment of dogs and owners gathered in the open area near the pond where class was conducted. Groups formed, broke apart, reformed. Most greetings were eagerly received, but sometimes–probably due to nervousness–an approach was ignored.

The dogs' owners socialized with each other, too.

The evening, the twenty-seventh of June, was summer at its classic best–warm with that unmistakably summer smell on the air. Just humid enough to make you feel close to the earth without feeling just plain close. If your skin perspired slightly, the breeze took care of it.

And under one of Linda's bushes, Chivas Beagle was making a personal contribution to the ecology. Didi held both the woven leather leash and her chin high, as if she were surveying the twenty or so other dogs and their owners from a greater distance than across Linda's yard.

"You're supposed to clean that up," I reminded her.

"With what?" she asked, as if this was the first time the problem arose.

"Scoop and paper bags–over there. Trash can–over there," I pointed out.

"Okay, people," Roxanne called to everyone, waving both chubby hands toward her. "Gather in."

Gretsky stood as far from the beagle poop as his six-foot leash would allow. Together we went and got the scoop and a paper bag and together we cleaned up after our friends.

"Just taking advantage of another opportunity," I explained to my pet. "This'll help us get into heaven."

Gretsky turned his nose away.

"Now let's divide up into groups of four," the young dog-training assistant told us. "Oh, here he is. Folks, this is Victor. He's going to demonstrate tonight with my dog, Marmaduke."

Marmaduke appeared to be a dolt of a boxer, but Victor was an interesting development. He was Karl and Linda's shared handyman–on overtime, I supposed. He still wore khaki and the straw hat, but they were grubbier than when I first saw them this morning, no doubt from all the car washing and lawn mowing. Yet he maintained a self-contained dignity.

Class began with the five groups of four walking our dogs in little circles, telling Biffy and Barkley and Spot to heel, hurry-hurry, stay, no stay, and lie down. That's *down*. Right.

Gretsky and I ended up farthest from Linda's house, toward the duckweed-covered pond. Didi and Chevy joined the group next to ours, and I noticed she rewarded little kibble-lips with something edible every time the dog did anything remotely right. I also caught her lifting the baby beagle up high enough to rub noses and wag tails in unison.

To Gretsky, eating has never been top priority. For him, communing with other living, breathing life forms was It. Three people in his eyesight at the same time constituted a party. A large gathering that included both his species and mine–beyond bliss. He wanted nothing so much as to greet each and every participant personally.

"Gretsky. *Gretsky,* heel," I begged. Together we headed around our team members, Martha and her black standard poodle, Jill, who were planted at the southern corner of our square. Gretsky caught sight of Barkley the Mutt in the neighboring group and sauntered toward him. "Barkley, ole buddy, ole boy, how ya doin'?" he seemed to say.

"Pay attention!" I admonished the social butterfly. "Heel." We made it around Martha and Jill only to encounter Bud and Dixie.

Gretsky ignored my admonition. "Oh, hi, Dixie," poke. "What're ya sittin' there for? Come on, let's make a break for it."

Dixie the Pomeranian hopped up and pranced around in a circumference of six inches until Bud reached down and put a stop to that.

"Sorry," I mumbled. More lost points. "Heel, Gretsky," and so on.

About half an hour into all this I became giddy. Maybe it was from watching Chevy wind twice around Didi's legs then get congratulated for sitting at her owner's left side when she ran out of leash.

Maybe it was from watching Victor the Handyman's expressionless face as he put Marmaduke the boxer through his paces.

Maybe it was from listening to Roxanne's earnest instructions delivered with his unfortunate lisp. My giddiness only worsened with the one-to-one brush-up lesson she stopped to give me. Apparently, my command voice needed work.

"Sit," she said like a no-nonsense nun ordering an auditorium full of rapscallions into their seats.

"Sit," I repeated dutifully.

"No, sit," she said again as if the rapscallions were hearing-impaired.

"Sit," I said with a bit more force.

"Like this," Roxanne alerted me and the rest of the class. "You've got to sound like you mean it. *Sit,*" she said, except as always it sounded like "thit."

"Gretsky, sit," I said, but by then it was impossible for me to keep a straight face. "Sorry. Sorry, Roxanne," I apologized while the rest of the class turned away or covered their mouths with their hands. "I'll have to practice that at home."

Roxanne's round cheeks were aflame. I wanted to assure her–truthfully–that I was giggling over my own ineptitude, but I was afraid my protestations would only embarrass her more. She had taken my laughter to heart, and nothing I might say would convince her otherwise.

Oh, dear, I thought. Oh, dear, dear, dear.

With a final glare in my direction the assistant trainer clapped her hands and moved away. "Okay, people," she called. "Form your starting line."

As we had been taught at the beginning of class, everyone lined up between two widely spaced holly bushes, Victor and Marmaduke included. Linda's somber stone house lay forward to our left with the tennis court and grape arbors beyond.

The flat green pond was nearer, a little to our right but still past where Roxanne stood twenty yards away. Aside from the grassy-green duckweed covering its surface, tall, picturesque grasses grew out of its banks. Most of the full-grown trees were around the distant edges of the property, and up above, the huge clear evening sky was just beginning to dim. I allowed myself to acknowledge the lovely, calm well-being only the out-of-doors can produce, a calm I probably wouldn't be experiencing tonight if I didn't have a dog.

"We're going to do something a little different this time," Roxanne informed us.

The exercise was a sit/stay with the owner walking twenty yards away before turning around for a recall. That meant dropping the leash–actually letting go of the dog–trusting him to stay put for fully half a minute until you could face him again, then trusting him to come to you rather than go anywhere else.

Marmaduke made it look easy. Roxanne folded her arms across her chest in an effort to appear complacent, but she positively beamed with pride.

To my right, tiny Dixie the Pomeranian did it, and Bud lowered himself to clowndom for both the recall and his congratulations when little four-legs arrived.

Next came Jill, the black standard poodle, parked expertly by Martha with a not-to-be-denied, "Jilly, sit," and, "Jilly, stay." Martha confidently strode her twenty paces, turned, and issued a girlish, "Jilly, *come"* accompanied by arms spread low for a hug.

Jilly pranced a crooked line that eventually made it into Martha's arms.

We were next. What the hell, I thought. Maybe peer pressure will have an effect.

"Gretsky, sit," I ordered my red-headed friend. "Gretsky, stay," I insisted, reinforcing the command with a flat hand square in front of his eyes and nose.

So far so good. I dropped the leash. I turned. I walked twenty yards. Out of the corner of my eye I saw Roxanne standing with her arms smugly folded–waiting.

I turned to face Gretsky, who–miraculously–also

waited.

"Gretsky, *come,*" I commanded even more eagerly than Bud, arms spread even wider than Martha's.

Gretsky was up. He was running toward me. Joy oh, joy, maybe this would be his crowning moment.

And then his I-don't-have-to-do-this! light bulb went on.

"Gretsky, come?" I muttered piteously as he cut an angle around me and dove straight into the pond. I hurried after him with Roxanne's smirk burning into my back.

Gretsky soon learned that swimming was hard work, especially with a wet leash in tow. After he turned around and swam back to the bank and allowed me to get my hands on said leash; after we finished the class with no remarks one way or the other from anyone, Didi summarized the situation as we loaded our dogs into my car.

"You know," she said, "if Linda doesn't come back, Gretsky might behave like this forever."

Chapter 11

WHEN I WENT out for the Friday paper, the leaves were dark and damp from an overnight rain and our driveway gave off a pungent wet-asphalt smell. Since the sky was an unrelieved dome of pale gray, I couldn't guess whether it would clear or get worse, but the *Philadelphia Inquirer* thought maybe intermittent showers.

"Terrific," I thought to myself, "I can slow down." Summer is never as undemanding or relaxing as its press releases suggest–give me the occasional rainy day.

As I was about to recreate my grocery list, the phone rang.

"Gin," Linda greeted me with distress in her voice. "Thank goodness you're there." She took a moment to gulp and breathe.

"What's wrong?" I asked.

"Oh, Gin. Something happened–I'm not sure what–Tibor growled or snapped at somebody, and now they don't want to wait out the quarantine. They want to put him down today."

"Doesn't a judge still have to rule on that?"

"I don't know. Oh, Gin. Can you please go over and talk to them? I'd go, but Bedoes still won't let me."

"Why not? You're out on bail. It's your dog."

"He doesn't want me anywhere near Tibor right now, so nobody can say I had any chance whatsoever to deprogram him."

"That's crazy."

"I know. But Bedoes says juries will seize on anything these days. Go there, Gin. Talk to those people. Tell them how well-trained Tibor is. Otherwise they're going to kill him."

"Wouldn't your employee–Victor–be better? He

knows Tibor, and Tibor knows him." I happened to be a bit wary of the animal myself.

"He won't do it. He hates speaking English to strangers, and he refuses to talk to cops."

"What do the police have to do with this?"

"Whoever called was some sort of officer. Please, Gin. Any delay might be too late."

I told her I'd do my best.

After we hung up, I phoned Alice, the woman at the PSPCA I'd spoken to before. She didn't know anything about this morning's incident with Tibor, but she promised to ask the man who complained to delay any action until I could get there to talk with him.

The directions took me east on the Schuylkill Expressway, then north on the Roosevelt Boulevard.

The Boulevard is not my favorite road. Lengths of it total twelve lanes north and south divided by three grassy, tree-planted median strips. Various signs alert you to crossovers and turns, but any lapse of concentration and I would be in Never-Never Land. Consequently, my grip on the wheel remained painfully tight.

Luckily, I switched strips in time to turn right on Whittaker without incident, perhaps because the mid-Friday-morning traffic was polite enough not to interfere.

A gentle rain began about then, and glimpses of brick row houses with white clapboard over the fire-line and irregular, antenna-topped roofs came in between swipes of my wipers. Buttonwood trees only slightly stunted by exhaust graced the sidewalks. A paunchy man wearing a polyester pullover shuffled quickly to and from the corner mailbox.

Over a crest the center-city skyline greeted me before a bit of industry obscured the view. This was North Philadelphia, some of it anyway, part of a vast area with a personality both forbidding and familiar. I knew of whole blocks where each fenced back yard tightly clutched its own round, above-ground pool–and sections where you kept driving even on a flat tire.

I made a left at St. Christopher's Hospital for Children, which looked like a pile of tan boxes labeled with a tall red sign on tall red legs.

Half a block later there were two broad retaining walls on either side of the street. My side was painted with a mural of dogs and cats, grass underfoot with mountains behind. Across the way what began as a Pennsylvania SPCA tribute on a pale ivory background had deteriorated into ordinary graffiti.

The organization's home sat on the right. Positioned behind three rows of parking was a low, modern brick building with inviting glass doors, but my destination was the original brick offices to the left. A rooster crowed as I got out of my car.

I shared the sidewalk with an old woman holding an umbrella over her wheezing bulldog. They seemed to be headed for the fairly active veterinary clinic inside– M.A.C., Mastercard, and Visa accepted. A sky-blue sign on the clinic's inner entrance reminded me that "Pets Need Dental Care, Too."

Sitting behind her boxy work station, a receptionist finished a client's paperwork before putting me in touch with Alice, then only seconds later my phone-mate emerged from a side hall to greet me.

"I had no idea you did so much here," I remarked as she led me through a wide doorway into the interior of the building. She was a brunette of about my height with long, fluffy hair and a brisk walk.

"Most people don't," she agreed. "They probably know about our adoption facility–through there." She waved a hand at a hallway of stacked cages leading to a door for the newer building. "The clinic, you saw. And we do flea dips all summer outside, except on damp days." She made a turn past some interior cubicles–tall cages with tile floors and raised tile pallets where the animals could keep clean and dry, all connected to outdoor runs. I hurried to keep up.

"But not many people are aware that for years we've had an 'animal control' contract with the city. Mostly we're supposed to pick up strays, but we also go along on police raids to handle drug dealers' guard dogs. We get called for cock fights and dog fights, too–whenever the police need help enforcing the anticruelty laws. Our Humane Police Officers are actually empowered by the state to make arrests.

"Well, here we are." She stopped in front of another bank of empty, freshly hosed cages and looked around expectantly. "I thought Lou would be here. Just a sec." She disappeared around the corner through a door. Then she poked her head back and told me, "This way."

Lou was outside with the dogs, perhaps waiting for the cage cleaner to finish. His eyes were locked with Tibor's, who was housed in the first run nearest the door. Perhaps ten other covered runs were connected to his. Almost every dog except Tibor appeared to be a pit bull.

I held the back of my hand against the wire mesh of his run. "Hi, there," I told him. "Remember me?" He sniffed my hand but continued to look past me toward Lou. His front paws shifted lightly like an athlete prepared to leap in any direction.

Alice, Lou, and I were sandwiched together on a side-walk between the runs and a high chain-link fence that surrounded a minor barnyard. The menagerie of chickens, ducks, and goats had mostly gathered under a lean-to to keep dry.

Lou wore brown slacks and a short-sleeved white shirt, which still gave the impression of a uniform. A control stick dangled from his belt. A few splotches of rain had dampened his shoulders, but for the moment the weather held back.

"Gin Barnes," I introduced myself.

"Lou Paciulan," he responded with an offer of his hand. Tibor made a low sound in his throat. Alice folded her arms and stood back to concentrate on our conversation, which we both knew could mean life or death for the German shepherd.

"I guess you heard that Linda Arden's attorney advised her not to come here herself, but she's very distressed about what happened and sent me to see what I could do to help."

Lou nodded. There were a couple of thick rolls of stubble under his chin. His eyebrows were black and wide, slanted now with sincerity and concern. He had laced his short, thick fingers together in front of his belt.

"So please tell me exactly what happened, and maybe we can see where to go from there."

"Well, Ms. Barnes, it's like this. I come in here to move 'im out for 'iz checkup, and before I opened up to get 'im, he growled and barked at me like he meant to go for my throat." The Humane Police Officer made a choke-hold gesture with his hand, then waved it away.

"Now ordinarily I don't get that from a bite case. Tell you the truth, most times we got pit bulls only go after other dogs. You get me? Now true, they're here on account of biting a person, but that is prob'ly just an exception." He gave Tibor a stare. "Now I ain't sayin' I'm afraid, 'cause I got experience and also I been bit and I come right back on the job. But those other dogs ain't killed a man, you get my drift?"

"Tibor's a very well-trained animal, Mr. Paciulan. He's won championships in obedience as well as in schutzhund."

"I hear you, Ms. Barnes, but now this schutzhund is what I'm worried about. And tell you the truth–I had 'im out before and he didn't do nothin' for me. Not nothin'." Lou shook his head and scowled. "It's too bad about Ms. Arden wantin' 'im back and all, but I ain't interested in bettin' my life on this one. Not me, thanks. If the judge gives the okay, I'll be the first one to say good riddance."

This was not anything I wanted to hear. I needed to stall so I could think how to correct all the misconceptions this man had acquired in such a hurry. Telling him Tibor had probably only been conditioned to attack his master's throat when given a certain signal–maybe a voice command, maybe one of those high-pitched dog whistles–would not help my cause. The better argument, the championships, had already failed to convince Lou about Tibor's competence.

"So what happened again?"

"I reached down to open the door..."

"No, no. Tell me everything. Was anybody else around? Did you say anything to Tibor?"

Lou tried to find his chin with his thumb and forefinger. "Nope. Just a regular morning. I'm leaning down, opening the door..."

"Did anybody say anything to you?"

He thought a minute. "Charlie mighta said hi."

Not much help, but I was still stalling for time, so I asked, "How did he say it–Hi, Lou? Hello? Good morning? What?"

"The usual, I guess. Just my name."

"Lou?"

"Naw. Pack-man. Short for Paciulan." Probably a throw-back to the popularity of the electronic game Pac-man.

And suddenly the idea came. The risk was enormous, but I certainly hadn't been making any headway with reason. So.

I gathered up my courage and prepared to do perfectly what I had bungled so badly the night before. I issued a command to a dog.

"*Packen,*" I told Tibor with all the authority my voice could muster.

Tibor growled and barked as if he wanted to eat his way out of the cage. Alice recoiled, and Lou visibly flinched.

"*Aus*" I commanded, and Tibor quieted immediately.

"What the h e l l ... L o u began, but I interrupted with a hearty, *"Platz!"*

Tibor dropped to his belly as if he'd been shot. Ears up like antennae, he awaited the next command as if we'd been working together all his life.

"Okay, *sitzl*" I said for good measure. I could hear the authority in my voice slipping, but like the champion he was, Tibor forgave my imperfection and sat up at the ready. *"So ist brave,"* I cooed at <u>him.</u> "Good dog."

Lou pinched his chin area and squinted his eyes.

Behind him Alice was buoyant. "What just happened?" she asked with glee in her eyes.

"Schutzhund commands are given in German, and they never use the dog's name first."

"So what's this *'packen'* mean?" the PSPCA spokesperson asked.

"I think that's the one for attack, but Tibor could only bark and growl because he was inside the cage. I think somebody calling out 'Pack-man' from across the room was probably all he needed to hear."

"Amazing."

"So, you see," I told Lou, "there's no reason why Tibor should give you a bit of trouble if you use his usual commands." Unless, of course, you stumbled upon the signal used by the human killer. "Will you at least keep him here for the full ten days?"

Lou squinted at me and shut his mouth with an effort "Okay, okay," he said "I ain't never seen anything like that. But you write me out a list, you hear? I don't wanna be saying that 'packen' thing when I mean sit down and shut up. You know?"

It wasn't quite as dramatic as walking away from an electric chair, but after Alice and I left Lou pondering his list of German schutzhund commands–written phonetically from memory as best I could–both of us women seemed joined by a common giddiness. "I was on your side," her manner seemed to say, "but it's my job to support Lou."

Aloud, she said, "Would you like to see Daisy?"

"Who's Daisy?" I asked.

"Our pig."

Housed about eye level in the hallway leading to the new building, Daisy was indeed a pig. She had exceptionally soulful eyes, was entirely black, and looked to be somewhere between a gym bag and a purse in size.

"We get quite a few pigs turned in," Alice told me as if this morning's drama had bonded us into best friends. "Ever since the item hit the newspapers–did you see it? The one about the six-hundred-pound pig our guys took out of some man's basement?"

"Must have missed it."

"Really? Well, it was in all the papers. They sedated the pig and put it on a stretcher. Then they removed a basement window and shoved him through it?" Alice still couldn't believe I had missed the story, so I shrugged an apology.

"Anyway, ever since, we've been getting lots of pigs turned in. They're illegal in the city, so we make sure they get adopted out of town. Cute, isn't she?"

"Darling." Was that pig spit on my shoulder? Yes, it

was. "Do you live out of town?" I inquired as I extracted a tissue from my purse.

Alice didn't get the joke at first. Then when she did, she laughed way too hard. Maybe she'd been an overly sheltered child or else she was a Starbucks fiend.

At the front door she wheeled and said, "That's all right then."

"Yes," I agreed. "Thanks for your help."

Tibor would remain in Lou's semi-capable hands for at least another seven days. Seven *short* days.

Chapter 12

I PHONED LINDA with the good news about Tibor before I left the parking lot of the PSPCA. Then at home when I heard the, "Please call at your convenience," message on my machine, I figured Timothy Bedoes had gotten the word from her and called to offer his congratulations.

Silly me. He wanted a favor: Dr. Fleming was flying in Sunday morning at 9:42–could I possibly spare the time to pick him up at the airport?

My various responsibilities paraded through my mind; but it was summer, after all, and the living was easy. "You can't do it?" I asked out of curiosity.

"I can if you can't," Bedoes responded hesitantly, "but he's quite eager to meet you, and I thought this seemed like a good opportunity..."

Perhaps the attorney didn't want to be bothered; but to give him his due, maybe he thought I, too, might be interested in meeting Dr. Fleming. If that happened to be the idea, for once he was right.

"Where does he need to be dropped off?" I asked.

"He's got a ten-thirty appointment. Can you take him there?"

"Where's there, Tim?"

"The morgue."

I should have guessed. A famous forensic pathologist comes in on a sensational dog-bite case, naturally his heart's desire would be to examine the evidence.

Suppressing a little shiver, I said, "Sure. I can do that."

Next, I phoned Rip at school to find out whether I was needed to entertain campers.

"Nope," he told me. "Stevie Luckenbill already

started. Great lead, babe. Thanks."

I smiled smugly into the receiver and suppressed a sigh of relief. Unless Rip wanted me to teach the kids how to rewire a lamp or change the oil in a car, I was short on ideas of what to do with them anyway.

And, of course, I had other plans for my day, i.e., visiting a hardware store. Not my new haunt, the huge Home Depot in King of Prussia, which is so customer-oriented they even offer a bridal registry. No, I needed the warmth of a sole-proprietorship like the one Akeesha told me Colin Greene owned.

Located on the main street of Norristown, it sported a straightforward green sign with raised gold lettering. Nearing noon as we were, the sun-covered cement of its parking lot smelled of warm dust and drying grass. Watching my feet was essential if I didn't want to trip on the broken paving.

The store's wide windows displayed Sputnik-shaped grills, American flags, plumbing parts, and spools of wire–in no discernible order. Jingle bells on a leather strip tacked to the screen door announced my entrance. The floor was a rolling expanse of hardwood aisles worn down the center with dark old finish and dust toward the edges. Metal bins of nails lined up along the center aisle. Scoops on a chain dangled at intervals, and a scale with a metal basket and dial hung at the end of the row. To the left stood labeled drawers of screws.

In front of the paint selection on the far right three customers in professional overalls waited for service from a sullen boy of about seventeen. He had straight dark hair, skin the color of tallow, and oval blue eyes. When he spoke to one of the customers, I noticed his large teeth had overlapped.

"Jakie," he shouted, and a matching boy of younger years scurried from the back room to do his brother's bidding.

I proceeded to the cross-wise counter protecting the boxes of tiny parts filling several rows of tall shelves from shoplifters. On the floor two elementary-school-aged boys were unpacking a crate and stuffing the contents onto a low display.

Daddy waited at the worn wooden counter, his own oval blue eyes staring with a proprietor's welcome. "What can I do you for?" he joked. His cotton summer shirt was brown plaid, wash-softened beyond need of an iron.

"Got any inch-and-a-quarter, cadmium-plated, annular-ring nails?"

"How many?" If my question raised one eyebrow hair, I must have missed it.

"Handful will do."

"Can getcha a dollar box."

"Perfect."

"By the way, were you by any chance Debbie Greene's father?"

The eyes blinked hard, but nothing else moved, not the care-worn shoulders, not the work-roughened hands spread on the smooth wooden counter. Yet Colin Greene's body discernibly tensed at the question, odd since my presence rarely put anyone on the alert.

"Yes, I was. Why do you ask?"

"Mr. Greene, you have my deepest sympathy." The mention of sympathy tilted the man's head and twisted his mouth.

"Oh, this is difficult," I said, and it was. Lying is never easy when you've had Cynthia and Donald Struve for parents.

However, practice makes perfect. "You see, my Amy suffers from anorexia nervosa, and Henry and I–Henry's my husband–we just weren't happy with Dr. Vogel, so we started asking around. That was when someone told us about your tragedy."

My aim had been to dispel any suspicions that I was a bill collector or process server–or cop–asap. Daddy Greene was a big strong man beneath those rounded shoulders, and he had a fire-and-brimstone look about him that inspired some concern.

And yet with all those children around, I felt safe enough physically. I needed to elicit the man's opinions on Karl Vogel, and the middle of a store was far too impersonal.

"Maybe you could offer me some advice," I began again with a glance around for other customers. "Is there anywhere we could talk, somewhere a little... quieter?" I didn't know whether Greene had any dog-training expertise, but with luck maybe I could find out.

"Ricky," he called. "Mind the register a minute." One of the urchins from the floor popped up and scurried around beside his father. Like his brothers, he appeared in need of sunlight and vegetables.

Without further words, Colin Greene showed me the way to a set of back stairs leading to a second-floor apartment A fifth small boy too old to be sucking his thumb was watching cartoons from an armchair.

The apartment was mainly a spacious great room with living area, dining table, and kitchen all together. Despite its size the room felt oppressively jammed with the furniture and paraphernalia necessary to a family of five boys and one man.

"My wife died in childbirth," Colin Greene offered either in explanation or apology while gesturing me into a dining-room chair. He opened the refrigerator, extracted a container of transparent green fluid, then proceeded to pour two tall glasses, one of which he set in front of me.

"Debbie might as well have been Jeremy here's

mother." He remained standing but jerked his chin toward the thumb-sucker in the overstuffed chair.

I sipped the green fluid. Mint tea, one hundred percent mint. Awful, but free if you grew your own.

"Debbie mothered all of them, really. Cooked. Ironed. Cleaned. Everything perfect like she knew she was headed for heaven, and she was getting herself ready." He took in a deep breath through his nose and let it out. "I miss her. I still do miss her. We all do."

Abruptly, he reached behind him and grabbed a framed photo off a shelf. In it the boys stood in a half circle around a softly rounded young girl sitting in a chair holding a baby. The girl beseeched the camera with her large oval eyes. She seemed infinitely unhappy. The rest of the kids looked entirely self-involved and needy.

Colin Greene stood sideways to the group with his head turned belligerently toward the camera, a stern taskmaster. I wondered when he had last smiled. Perhaps back before the baby Jeremy was born. Three, four years. My heart hurt just imagining his grief.

"How old was she, Mr. Greene?"

"When she died? Fifteen. Thirteen when she begged me to see that charlatan Vogel about her weight. Her friend was going, and she wouldn't let up about it until I let her go, too." Greene shook his head at the ceiling. "She wasn't right from then on, and there wasn't a thing anybody could do."

"What did Vogel say about your daughter?"

Greene pushed his glass away and tightened his face as if to prevent tears. "Said she was unconsciously trying to stay a child. Now I ask you, how could he say that when she was doing such a great job taking care of us? Willingly, mind you. I wasn't holding any whip over her head."

Not much you weren't. I just met the man and already

I could hear his unspoken expectations, see how he had taken it for granted Debbie would shoulder the responsibilities of her deceased mother. When I glanced at her photograph a second time, I could almost hear her screaming for relief.

"Bunch of self-serving doctor talk, if you ask me," her father muttered. "Trying to make me forget the wrong ideas he put in her head."

Suddenly Colin Greene's intensity hit me full force. "Get your daughter away from that evil man," he bellowed.

Then just as suddenly his face writhed with hard memories and his fist twisted into his forehead.

Was it possible this man was unaware of Karl's death? I glanced around–not a newspaper in sight, the television set tuned to a children's station. Improbable, but possible. "Vogel's dead, haven't you heard?"

Greene did not reply. He just glared at me.

I waited for him to resume breathing before I said, "You've been very helpful. I'll just let myself out."

Since I hadn't really wanted the nails, I breezed by young Ricky without mentioning them. He was busy playing penny football with his brother anyway.

Unfortunately, I was all the way to my car before I realized I hadn't asked any dog questions. The fact that there had been no pets of any sort in the apartment meant nothing considering its size.

Of course, I had exited the store through an extensive selection of electrical parts and equipment...

Chapter 13

I FIGURED picnicking with my kids, and hopefully Rip, might be a sneaky but pleasant way to see how Stevie Luckenbill was working out. So, on the way back from Colin Greene's hardware store I picked up two corned-beef sandwiches on rye with cole slaw, no Russian dressing on mine, nothing to drink. I could stand the "bug juice" they served at camp if everybody else could.

According to Joanne Henry, Rip's ultra-efficient secretary, my husband was occupied interviewing a teaching applicant, who was there on his lunch break from some nine-to-five job in industry.

Since I knew the transition from industry to teaching wasn't nearly as simple as most people think, I asked Joanne to estimate the applicant's chances, whispering because I wasn't entirely positive Rip's door was soundproof.

"Twenty/eighty," she whispered back. Her beige hair never moved when she spoke, but her glasses bobbed up and down on her nose. She wore a sleeveless summer dress as tailored and flattering on her middle-aged frame as all the rest she owned.

"I'd have guessed thirty/seventy."

"I met him," Joanne replied with a wink.

A pity. I hated to think of anyone's ambitions being thwarted. Rip did, too, which was why I knew he would take the whole lunch hour to counsel with the young man. I left Rip's sandwich and pickle with Joanne.

The sky was dotted with cotton balls dusted lavender. Still the noontime sun made me wriggle on the dark-green picnic-table bench. Chelsea treated me to a "Hi, Mom/Bye, Mom," kiss, swinging her legs out from under the table simultaneously as I sat down. I caught sight of Garry flapping his arms and trotting downhill toward the tetherball. So much for a family picnic.

Stevie Luckenbill? Elsewhere.

Across the table from me Harvey Serrentino, Bryn Derwyn's Spanish teacher, contemplated the last of what appeared to be ham and cheese on a roll. His forty-inch shoulders tested the seams of a white Bryn Derwyn staff shirt. His nose was lumpy as ever, his light brown hair still thick with waves. Harvey's features were so irregular he was cute. I assumed he was able to linger over his lunch because summer school classes ended at noon and tutoring was done by appointment.

"You meet Stevie Luckenbill yet?" I inquired.

He tucked a flap of ham back into his kaiser roll. "Did you know it takes twenty-five hundred gallons of water to support a meat-eater every day? That's just water related to his food–my food–raising the grain to feed the animals, slaughtering the pig that died to make this sandwich, that sort of thing."

"No, I didn't."

"Yes. A vegetarian's food only requires three hundred gallons of water a day."

This lunch was giving me heartburn, and I hadn't even unwrapped my corned beef.

"Also–since you did so poorly on the previous question–I don't suppose you were aware there are ninety-five percent fewer species of songbirds in the American West than a hundred years ago because thoughtless people like you and me cleared farmland to support our carnivorous habit?"

I was this close to asking Harvey why he was lecturing me when all I wanted to know was whether he had met Stevie Luckenbill.

Then I realized he had already answered my question.

Despite Harvey's strong disincentive, my sandwich

was delicious. I even drank three cups of pink bug juice—maybe because all the talk about water made me thirsty.

Then I went inside and borrowed Joanne's phone.

Of Akeesha's leads, Annie Snellenberg wasn't home and had no answering machine. Darlene Polk put me off, claiming she couldn't be interrupted at work and would be gone all day Saturday at "the coursing championships," whatever they were.

Akeesha had also supplied me with her predecessor's phone number and address, and Nancy Carlino answered on the second ring.

"Oh," I said. "How lucky to find you home."

The woman Karl had fired snorted into her phone. "I got no job. Where the hell would I be?"

I told her my name and asked if she could spare a few minutes to talk to me. As expected, she asked me why. Except I believe she phrased it, "What the hell for?"

"I'm trying to save Dr. Vogel's dog," I replied as planned, figuring part of the truth might be bizarre enough to arouse Nancy Carlino's curiosity.

"Ha," she barked in my ear. "Come ahead. This I got to hear."

While concentrating on my objective I had forgotten where I was and who I was with. Now I hung up the phone and caught sight of Joanne Henry's expression. Her lips were a squiggle of disapproval, her eyes a blank stare of disbelief.

"What, may I ask, was that all about?"

"Just doing a favor for a friend."

"And is this favor going to get us in the newspapers again?" Rip's secretary had been the one to educate me about how private schools remain afloat on a sea of good-will. Bad press was as deadly as a torpedo.

The day she originally imparted that information Bryn Derwyn had just been hit. Our attorney, Richard

Wharton, had been found–by me–murdered in the school's community room. Joanne kept me from telling any number of reporters exactly what they could do with their noses.

Faced with her don't-even-try-it expression, I shelved the long, mitigating explanation I had been assembling. "No newspapers," I said, "just a favor for a friend."

Joanne's eyes rolled.

"Chardonnay and an explanation when it's over," I promised.

"But of course," she agreed. We had discovered we were on the same team–Rip's–over a bit too much chardonnay at my first faculty party.

"Go forth and multiply," she remarked as she turned back to her computer.

Nancy Carlino's apartment encompassed the second floor of a house on Tallymore Road in Berwyn. Finding it required a couple trips around the block because the traffic moved too quickly for reading house numbers. Also, an elderly man in long sleeves and gray cotton work pants fussed around the front yard as if he owned the place. After I realized Nancy probably only rented the second floor, I figured maybe he *did* own the place; but it took me a couple of passes to figure that out.

Nancy's rooms were accessible only from the inside stairway or via a fire escape attached to the back. I opted for the inside stairs.

Her living room lay to the right of the upper landing. Sunlight invaded the four huge casement windows and sucked the color out of the furnishings.

"So," Nancy greeted me. "What's this nonsense about saving Vogel's dog?" The way she spoke Karl's name reminded me she had worked for him less than a year ago and her dismissal, supposedly based on her appearance, had prompted a discrimination lawsuit.

Discreetly, I tried to form my own opinion. She *was* a big woman, tall as well as overweight. The elastic grooves from her underwear showed through her man's white T-shirt and gray bicycle shorts. She wore pink scuffles, carefully applied eye makeup, and earrings each consisting of several blue hoops and a gold lightning bolt.

Her black hair probably reached her chin, but it coiled back to her ears. The style was not especially flattering, but that may have been the fault of her face. At the moment the woman looked irascible.

"May I come in?" I asked. Standing in her hall doorway, cool air swirled around our feet.

"Oh, yeah," she said, snapping out of her examination of me. "Come in. Sit." She shut the door and the air-conditioner swiftly raised goose bumps. I vigorously rubbed them down on my arms and legs while I selected a chair, a padded rattan one not so marshmallowy looking as the other two. The sofa– forget it. The sofa looked as if it would swallow me: cause of death–peony-print asphyxiation.

Nancy sat on the edge of another, larger chair.

Not knowing how long this aggressive woman would tolerate me, I got straight to the point. "To answer your question," I said, "Linda Arden is afraid they'll put Tibor down at the end of his rabies quarantine, and she asked me to do what I could to prevent that."

"And?"

"And so I'm exploring a few ideas about how Karl's death might have occurred other than what the police think happened."

"Which is?"

"They think Linda retrained Tibor to attack Karl." Nancy Carlino laughed, not an especially infectious sound, so I wasn't tempted to join in. When she finished, she said, "Good Lord, saving a dog. Now I've heard everything. Not that I wouldn't like to see Karl's mutt live out the life of Riley–hell, he only did what most of the man's clients could only dream–but I can't say I understand what you're getting at about Linda."

I gulped, realizing this conversation might be over in a hurry. "The PSPCA will only release Tibor to Linda, but not if she was the one who trained him to bite."

"What do you think happened? Somebody else re-trained him?"

"Possibly."

The next laugh was brief and contained even less humor. "And you suspect me. Isn't that why you're here?"

"Not exactly. I thought as a former employee you might know of someone…"

"Oh, don't give me that crap. I don't know why the hell you're helping Karl Vogel's ex-wife, and I don't especially care; but you're barking up the wrong tree, sister. Because I had every reason to want Karl Vogel alive."

I waited, an excellent interrogation technique, or so I've heard.

After a moment, Nancy Carlino sighed and leaned down on her knees. Above bulging cheeks her eyes lifted to confide in mine.

"Look at me," she invited. She spread her arms and straightened her back, the better for me to view her torso. Then she slouched down on her knees again. "I gained eighty pounds working for 'Doctor' Karl Vogel. All that talk about food day in and day out. Hell, I couldn't wait for lunch hour–so I didn't."

And then what happened? I asked with my eyebrow. "Karl fired me."

"Just like that?"

"No. No, of course not. First he gave me the You're-a-valuable-person/you-can-do-it spiel."

"He wanted to help you lose the weight?"

"You bet he did. What do you think those clients thought when they walked into his office and saw me? It was like wearing a billboard: Abandon all hope, ye who enter. Karl was in quite a pickle. He couldn't fire me because of how I looked, but he couldn't keep me either.

"He started working on my mind. Told me I was wonderful, a great office manager, that I was gold clear through, and he cared about my welfare." She paused to reflect. Then she looked me in the eye again. "I figured if I was really so wonderful and valuable, how I looked was insignificant, so why bother losing the weight?" Good point.

"What about the health issues?"

Nancy shrugged. "I do those stairs. I walk. I clean. Could be worse."

"You ever express your views to any of Karl's clients?" Nancy Carlino blushed to the roots of her curly black hair. "Yeah. Yeah, I did. But just the ones who needed to hear it. You know?"

I thought I did know, if she meant the ones to whom everyday life was an overwhelming struggle, who found even a modest amount of confidence an impossible goal to attain. I've wanted to nurture a few of those ailing egos myself until they could find the first rung of the ladder by themselves. But I never even tried. Nancy Carlino had tried, and I admired her for that.

The only thing she did wrong was to interfere with somebody else's livelihood.

"Tell me about the lawsuit."

Another shrug. "When Karl fired me, I realized everything he said was just bullshit. He wasn't anybody's guru. He was just a smoke-and-mirrors wizard playing mental games with unsuspecting fools. If the fools tricked themselves into losing some weight, they believed he was responsible. When they failed, they blamed themselves.

"At first I didn't act on my anger. I just went about the business of trying to find another job. That's when I discovered what people really think of fat. Most people anyway. The prejudice is real, girl. Don't kid yourself. Prospective employers give me all sorts of carefully worded–unactionable–excuses, but I can see the rejection on their faces the minute I walk into an interview." She wagged her head. "I've got a college degree, experience. I am a good office manager, but I'll be lucky to land a job as a filing clerk."

I wanted to apologize for the world, to offer warm fuzzies, to help her find a job; but Nancy's ego seemed just as healthy as her outlook, so I just sat back and listened.

"One night I was out with some friends, drinking, and I went on and on about employer prejudice and how I lost my job with Karl, until one of the guys–a lawyer as it happened–asked me why I didn't file a discrimination suit. We talked it over for a week or so, and I decided to go for it."

"Now that Karl's dead, is that the end of it?"

"We hit some snags anyway, but yes. There wasn't enough to be gained–justice maybe, but you can't eat justice. And to get it would have cost more than I can afford."

"I'm sorry."

"Oh, shit. I'll think of something." She rose to usher me out.

I almost said, "Nice meeting you," at the door but remembered my negligence with Colin Greene just in time.

"You ever have a dog?" I asked.

Nancy Carlino was too savvy to give me that one easily.

"Why?" she said. "You have one you want to get rid of?"

Chapter 14

RATHER THAN linger in Nancy Carlino's driveway, I paused in the parking lot of an Acme market to try Annie Snellenberg on my cell phone. Again, Karl's disgruntled client did not answer; but the afternoon was young, so I decided to go the half hour out of my way and at least get an impression of her surroundings. Then if I ever reached her, I might have a handle on my approach.

Annie's neighborhood was accessed by a bridge across the Schuylkill River, and therefore could no longer be considered Main Line–it was serviced by an entirely different railroad line and had no national image to uphold.

Actually, her block wasn't doing such a good job of upholding anything. Iron bars graced at least half the front windows. Most doors remained shut tight despite the warmish summer day. Most of the houses were fraternal twins, never identical, as if the buildings scarcely tolerated being joined porch to roof and refused to agree on anything more.

The front yards on Annie's side of the street sloped uphill with maybe eight feet from sidewalk to porch. Her half yard was planted thickly with a struggling assortment of greenery going to seed. The neighbor's was adorned by grass.

I parked at the curb and leaned against the Subaru's fender wondering what, if anything, to do. Knocking on Annie's door seemed reasonable, but when that went un-answered, I decided to look in the front window, which was unbarred and only veiled on the bottom half with white lace. Shielding my eyes, I could make out a living room with a broken-down, slipcovered sofa, a small television, a TV table, and about three cats–no dog.

"Can 1 help you?" a voice called from the sidewalk. Female. Young. Protective.

My heart galloped. Rudely staring into strangers' windows is uncomfortable enough without being caught.

"I'm looking for Annie Snellenberg," I told the woman, who wore a white shirt tucked into cutoff jeans. Blond hair, dark-framed glasses. For the occasion she was pretending to be tough, but even from the porch I could see the effort was a stretch.

I rejoined her on the sidewalk and introduced myself. Her name was Carol.

"Do you know Annie?" she asked, still suspicious I might be a thief or worse, some sort of salesperson.

"Not really. I'm just doing a favor for a friend. Do you know her well?"

"Just well enough to look out for her," the blonde replied. "We've had a lot of break-ins around here lately, so we got in the habit of watching each other's houses. Mostly Annie keeps to herself, but now and then we talk."

"Then maybe you can help me," I suggested. "Do you have any idea where she is?"

"Work. She's a dispatcher for a construction company seven to three. She should be home soon." Annie had not been employed the last time she saw Karl, as far as Akeesha knew.

"Great. Do you happen to know anything about her experiences with a diet doctor named Karl Vogel?"

"Why?" Carol asked warily.

In broad terms I explained about Karl's death. Then I said, "I'm helping Ms. Arden's attorney rule out other suspects."

Annie's neighbor clutched her collar and stepped away staring. "Annie can't be a suspect."

"Why not?"

"That's preposterous. Just plain preposterous."

"Why? That's what I'm here to learn."

"You'd just have to look at her. Annie couldn't hurt anyone. She just wouldn't…"

"Have you got a minute? Can we sit down here?" Carol allowed me to steer her to a shady spot on the curb in front of my car. We perched there with our bare knees up like girls getting ready to play jacks.

"What was the doctor's name again?" she asked.

I told her.

"Doesn't sound familiar, but it had to be him," she replied thoughtfully.

"Then she told you something?"

Carol nodded, pushed her glasses up to the bridge of her nose, folded her hands on her knees. "Back when she wasn't working, she sometimes spent whole days just hating some guy. Obsessing about him, you know? I thought it had to be a boyfriend, but maybe it was your diet doctor. Whatsizname, Karl."

"What did she say about him?"

"That it wasn't fair. That he gave her high hopes and then really let her down. She was seriously bummed out, let me tell you. Somebody, a sister I think, finally got her treated for depression. She's got that tendency anyway, you know?"

"Is she better now?"

Carol shrugged. "How can you be sure with something like that? She's no thinner, I can tell you that.

"Humph," she said, "For a while there I thought she was making it up, you know? She sure glowed when she talked about that guy." Carol shook her head. "But I couldn't imagine where they met, and I never saw anybody come to the house, you know? Her diet doctor. Makes sense."

Annie's neighbor seemed consummately satisfied, as if one of life's rules had been upheld: Fat women can't have boyfriends, just disappointing diet doctors. My heart ached for Annie Snellenberg.

And then she pulled into her driveway and broke my heart completely.

She parked her large sedan, an elderly Ford was my guess, close to the garage door at the end of the drive. Extracting her bulk from the vehicle took perhaps ten times longer than for a smaller person, and the effort raised a sweat.

"See ya," Carol told me as she rose from the curb. Apparently she preferred not to be there when I confronted Annie. Or perhaps she had a load of wash she urgently needed to switch to the dryer. Either way, she was halfway across the street before I could thank her for her help.

Annie slowly progressed down the drive. Each step appeared to hurt her feet, perhaps also chafe her legs painfully together. Placing her backless rubber-soled sandals took all her concentration. She did not notice me.

Karl's disappointed patient wore a pale pink dress sparsely covered with rosebuds. "Gather ye rosebuds while ye may," popped unbidden into my mind followed by the phrase, "unrequited love." Annie Snellenberg had fallen in love with a man who promised to release the capable and confident thin person inside her. When the glow of his promises tarnished, her self-hatred had deflected onto him, however briefly. Standing at her side door, leaning forward to insert a key in the lock, she appeared to me to be a three-hundred-pound shell.

I did not introduce myself.

Rather, feeling helpless and distressed, I wanted to hurry home to re-center myself, to shamelessly hide out until I was ready to cope again.

So that's exactly what I did.

Chapter 15

"GRETSKY RAN away," Garry greeted me.

Reality had forced me to shake off my Annie Snellenberg distress. The Barnes family needed to eat, so I needed to shop. Availing myself of one of those many Acmes, I bought $120 worth of food in thirty minutes, paid with a credit card, and drove mechanically home through the summer's earlier rush hour.

Garry's announcement cleared away any lingering reflections and instantly put me back in gear.

"When?"

"About five minutes ago. We opened the door, and he bolted."

Apparently, the pressure of Gretsky's naughtiness had had too long to build up. Probably my fault for leaving him alone.

"Hop in the car."

"Dad and Chelsea just went."

"So we'll go, too." If Gretsky returned, unlikely as it was, we would eventually come home and find him. If someone phoned about him, the answering machine would take the message.

We guessed that Rip and Chelsea turned left at the end of Beech Tree Lane–Gretsky's favorite direction. The neighborhood just east of us offered a slightly denser array of streets and houses. Ours was a very gregarious dog.

So Garry and I turned west and meandered through the awkward turns of that neighborhood. Windows down, we shouted the miscreant's name into the yards of strangers. Alternately, we listened for barking–Gretsky usually ran until he made a new friend. You might say he made friends at about twenty-five miles an hour.

Nothing. Half an hour later we crossed paths with Rip, stopped to commiserate, and agreed we should all go home. Chelsea pouted and averted her face. In the front seat of my car Garry silently cried, and I struggled to contain my panic.

The blinking light on our answering machine raised a unanimous cheer.

"Hush," Rip admonished us. "Listen." He pressed the play button and a cheery woman who identified herself as Mrs. Beck told us she had our dog, to please call 555-1728.

Rip dialed. The rest of us watched his face and listened longer than seemed necessary under the circumstances. Eventually, Rip said, "I guess so, if you're really sure." More talk from the other end. Rip finally took down an address and hung up the phone.

Looking mildly incredulous, he told us, "Gretsky's playing with their dog and their three-year-old son, and they're having so much fun she invited Gretsky to stay another hour."

In my head I sputtered and swore. "Are you saying that while the four of us were scouring the neighborhood worried sick, Gretsky was having a...party?"

"That's about it."

I waved my arms with disgust. "Kids, bring in the groceries. Rip, set the table. I'll make dinner." Rip gave me a bemused smile and reached for the flatware.

While I fried frozen minute-steak meat and sliced long rolls, Garry slipped in behind me and placed a box under the kitchen sink.

"What's that?" I asked.

"Tell you later."

We all sat down to cheesesteaks and tried not to resent our dog's amazing luck.

"Do we have any old magazines or newspapers I

could cut up?" Chelsea asked. The leftover kinks from a home permanent were growing out of her ear-length, golden-red hair, hopefully in time to begin eighth grade in the fall. Just last month I had been persuaded to allow the use of mascara, a brown that wouldn't look too harsh against her tan but made her deep brown eyes astonishingly dramatic and mature. She had argued that as a Counselor-in-Training, she *needed* to look mature.

In truth she was looking more and more adult anyway, and the makeup was merely an acceptance of the fact. Recently she had grown taller, rounder, and more beautiful than even a mother guessed was possible. Scary. Very scary. Fortunately, she was still oblivious to her new effect on boys. Dad monitored that every day, watching for any change.

"Sure," I answered. "I'll help you find some after dinner. What do you need them for?"

"A project for Stevie."

Interesting. Perhaps I would get the details later. In the meantime, what was that smell?

Rip had noticed it, too, but his thoughts went in another direction. He addressed Garry. "You know anything about the boys' room at school?"

The indelicate question seemed to make our son squirm, but he lifted his chin and replied, "We're saving the world, Dad."

"By not flushing the toilets?"

"Yes," Chelsea said in defense of her brother, a possible first. "Conserving water. The girls are doing it, too."

. "Well, tell them to save the world some other way. We can't have the school smelling like a latrine."

Garry and Chelsea exchanged dismayed glances.

"Stevie's idea, I suppose?" Rip inquired.

The children all but panicked.

Their father set down his sandwich. "Look," he said. "Stevie's not in trouble. I just want everybody to start flushing the toilets again, okay? I'll talk to her about it on Monday."

The tension in the kids drained away, and they resumed eating.

"What is that smell?" I asked.

Rip shrugged. The kids studied their plates.

I stood up and sniffed, trying to locate the source of the odor. My nose took me to the kitchen–to the cabinet under the sink.

"Garry! What is this?"

Through the pass-through to the plank table, I could see our son's face perk up.

"Isn't it cool? It's a compost box for garbage."

"It seems to be full of worms." Just what I wanted in my kitchen, a wooden box full of mud, worms, and garbage.

Garry came to my side, smiling proudly. "Stevie said I did a great job finding enough worms. She says it doesn't work nearly as fast if you don't get enough."

"Did she tell you to put it under the sink?"

"No, that was my idea. It's a garbage disposal–get it?"

"Out. Outside. Find a place far away from the house. Okay?"

Garry's smile faded briefly but immediately returned. "You're gonna try it? You're really gonna?"

"No. You'll try it. I give you the garbage–you put it in the box."

"Cool." He lifted the box out of my hands and carried it toward the front door.

"Somewhere where Gretsky can't get to it," I shouted after him.

Gretsky. It was time to pick up the party-boy.

My Saturday morning started sooner than expected–

5:30 a.m. to be exact. Whenever the dog ate his dinner late, he needed to go out early.

No," I said when he poked my arm. "Go lie down."

The Great One licked my elbow.

I tucked my arm under the covers and rolled away from him.

Gretsky flicked the covers out of the way with his snout, then pressed his cold nose against an exposed patch of skin.

Cold nose. On my warm back. I jumped three inches off the bed.

"Gretsky, dammit." I sat up with my legs over the edge and glared at him. He had the sense to look pathetic.

"Oh, all right" I conceded, and June 29th was underway. Shivering by an open door in my nightie waiting for our dog to come back inside always wakes me up for the duration.

Over coffee I flipped through the magazines Chelsea had stayed up to read. A black-and-white ad showing a svelte young woman in a floor-length sheath caught my eye. Arms folded across her chest she stared frankly into the camera. Her hair shone. Her expression said, "I dare you," and her body said, "I'm perfect/I can wear anything."

For incentive I tore out the picture and stuck it to the refrigerator with a magnet.

At eleven Chelsea wandered into the kitchen and asked me why I had a picture of Angela Muldoon on the refrigerator.

Pride prevented me from admitting I wanted to emulate her body shape by subconscious suggestion. With her on the refrigerator just maybe I would reach for the no-fat yogurt instead of the potato salad.

"Don't you think she's pretty?" I hedged.

"Well, yeah," Chelsea agreed. "But she's only twelve

years old. I'm already bigger than her."

I examined the photo more closely. My thirteen-year-old sage was right; there was a reason for those folded arms. I felt duped, manipulated, and annoyed. Talk about your unobtainable goals! As soon as Chelsea finished her Frosted Mini-Wheats and went to get dressed, I crumbled Baby-face Muldoon up in a ball and threw her in the wastebasket.

Then I settled down with a second cup of black coffee and flipped through the clippings Chelsea had handed me before she left. Many appeared to have come from an old stack of newspapers she found in the garage.

They were all about animals. Articles about braces for your dog's teeth, a camp for you and your dog to attend together, and one about a female detective who specialized in finding stolen pets.

Other articles reported examples of abuse: an Ann Landers column regarding four boys who killed a cat, the sentencing of the men who caused a local sensation when they set a pit bull on a dalmatian, and another story about three men arrested for staging dog fights in a basement in North Philadelphia. I read these through with both fascination and distaste, sorry to be aware of such horrors, particularly sorry to be closely involved with a story so similar.

The offbeat articles appealed to me more: a landfill location rejected because it threatened the habitat of certain marbled salamanders, a North Carolina town suspicious about the politics behind the placement of some offensive hog farms. In the magazine *Entertainment Weekly,* actress Sigourney Weaver remarked to columnist Stephen Schaefer about the ants crawling all over her in the film *Copycat.* "…we couldn't kill any of them," she said, because the owner wanted them all back.

Perhaps the most poignant was another old Ann

Landers, a wrapup of responses to a column about the $16,000 vet bill after a dog had been dragged three-quarters of a mile behind a pickup truck. "From San Jose...Most of my adult life I have been abused by cruel, insensitive bosses, family members who did not approve of the way I was living my life, rude salespeople, smart-mouthed teens, and men who belittled and insulted me because I was not thin and beautiful.... My only friend, who has always been there for me, making me feel beautiful and loved and protecting me from harm, is my dog."

Maybe peeking in windows wasn't a good thing to do, but I was awfully glad to know Annie Snellenberg owned cats.

Still with only a vague idea of the project Stevie had inspired, I set the clippings aside and picked up today's paper. One of Darlene Polk's excuses for not talking to me had been an all-day lure coursing event she planned to attend. If I could find it listed in the paper, maybe I could find her.

"Want to go?" I asked when Chelsea, freshly showered and dressed, wandered by the table.

"Meeting Sarah at the mall," she replied.

Garry had been invited to swim in a friend's pool.

"What is it?" Rip asked over the edge of the sports section.

"Dogs running around, as near as I can tell."

"Grass needs mowing," he replied.

Oh, goodie. I got to drive to a field in New Jersey all by myself.

"What about me?" Gretsky asked with his eyes.

"In your dreams, buddy," I told him. "In your dreams."

There were two fields, actually, set behind a school in Burlington County, New Jersey, Nobody fought me for a parking space along the gravel lane. Nobody said boo to me as I strolled past the few trailers, which obviously served as housing for long-distance travelers. Tarp canopies shaded folding chairs and dog crates. I noticed at least one used charcoal grill.

Most of the vehicles lined up against a gully full of scrub trees were boxy station wagons suitable for transporting tall dogs. Past the gully lay some widely striped yellow and white tents pitched at the base of the nearest field. Beyond a space for pedestrians were more vehicles, including a quilted stainless-steel refreshment truck selling hot food, and a small U-Haul truck, its side taped with pages of the results of the day's various events.

I wandered into the shade of an open tent and made use of one of the many empty chairs. A woman named Marla also sat there killing time with her saluki, a placid pooch with an impossibly pointy nose, a pale face, and some stringy black hair. Marla was kind enough to answer my ignorant questions.

"You see the white plastic bag out there?" She pointed up the gently sloping hill. "It's attached to a wire that's attached to a motor. The motor pulls the pretend rabbit– the plastic bag–around the field in a certain pattern and the dogs follow it. Judges watch for speed, endurance, agility, enthusiasm, and follow."

"The dogs don't care that it isn't a real rabbit?"

"See for yourself," Marla suggested. As we watched, a starter hollered, "Tally-ho," and a trio of short, skinny whippets wearing red, yellow, and blue set off at perhaps forty miles an hour after the even-faster-moving plastic bag. When the bag abruptly switched angles, the dogs adjusted their course with varying skill.

"Wow," I said, shaking my head in amazement at their speed. Pound for pound, whippets were apparently the fastest of all the sighthounds.

"What I like best," Marla confided with a grin, "is that coursing is all the dogs. There isn't one thing an owner can do to improve their performance."

I thought about the schutzhund practice I'd seen. Although lure coursing essentially made use of what sighthounds were bred to do, schutzhund disciplined the innate abilities of its breeds for use by humans. In contrast, coursing seemed much more frivolous, perhaps more purely a hobby.

The people involved evidenced interesting differences, too, the same way a suntan once indicated the wearer was working class and now advertised that we'd been on vacation. I supposed my experimental home repairs and collection of "fast and easy" cookbooks also revealed plenty about me.

The real question was, "What was I learning about Darlene Polk?" So far, only that she probably had no more dog-training experience than most of the rest of us.

I asked Marla if she knew the woman. She stood up and stepped out into the sun, shielding her eyes with her hand as if saluting the next tent. "Over there," she indicated with a wave. "The one with the greyhound."

"Standing or sitting?"

"Sitting."

I thanked the woman profusely and made my way over to the second tent.

Nuts to the image of the jolly fat person–I connect obesity with sorrow and pain, perhaps an underlying health problem before, certainly after. Almost never to sloth or neglect. I felt sorry for the person in direct proportion to how sorry they felt for themselves.

Darlene Polk's wet eyes were very sad indeed. A graceful hand reached out to stroke her greyhound's sleek neck. The gesture reminded me of someone checking her limbs after an accident, the flicker of relief on the woman's face similar to the surprise of waking up yet another morning. Even before I spoke to Darlene Polk it seemed obvious she had transferred her self-image onto her pet, perhaps even lived out her fantasies through the slender, nimble animal.

It occurred to me that every greyhound I ever met had been rescued from the dog-racing industry.

"Is your dog rescued by any chance?" I asked politely.

Darlene Polk raised her rheumy eyes in my direction. They were blue. Her hair was thin and formerly black, now a bun of woolen gray. She wore a limp, yellow cotton housedress over her bulk, no stockings, and black cloth shoes with Mary Jane straps. Varicose veins in both blue and purple traced their way between bumps of cellulite.

"Oh, yes. Swifti's rescued. Why do you ask?"

I sat down across from the sweet-faced tan dog. His head rose higher than my lap. His humanlike eyes regarded me needily.

"Because I know of someone who might like a greyhound, and I thought you might be able to tell me how to get one."

Darlene rummaged in an open canvas bag and extracted a brochure for The Greyhound Protection League, which appeared to be based in Palo Alto, California.

Before my fib grew too unwieldy, I decided to turn it into the truth. Nancy Carlino lived alone in a house with a yard. She hadn't answered me one way or the other about whether she wanted a dog–*"Why? Do you have one you want to get rid of?"*–but I liked the idea of putting her together with Darlene, no matter what. Nancy was content with herself and her size.

"Isn't there anyone more local?" I asked. "This woman lives in Pennsylvania."

"I got mine through Make Peace with Animals in New

Hope," she told me. "But I don't have the number with me.

New Hope, Pennsylvania. "Perfect," I exclaimed. "May I have her call you?"

"Sure." Darlene still seemed bewildered that I had approached her. Now she blinked and twitched her graceful hands while I wrote her phone number on the back of the brochure she had given me.

"Thanks," I said. "Did Swifti race yet?"

She shook her head, turned back to watch the borzois who were presently running.

No way of redirecting the conversation onto Karl Vogel seemed possible, not without seriously disillusioning the woman or perhaps frightening her, so I decided to be content with what I had already learned.

Darlene Polk may well have had reason to hate the renowned nutritionist, but she did not appear to possess enough ego or enough initiative to take Tibor out of his dog run at night and retrain him–with force–to kill.

That, at least, was my first impression; and probably nothing Darlene could say to me just then would have convinced me otherwise.

A trained therapist, I was not.

Chapter 16

I BOUGHT AN ice cream cone and loitered around the lure-coursing competition another hour, watching Rhodesian ridgebacks and Afghan hounds, Scottish deerhounds and Irish wolfhounds, even Swifti the greyhound, chase that silly plastic bag until finally the whole business started to look like an instant replay.

Except for when she needed to start Swifti, while I was there Darlene Polk never budged from her folding chair. A very sedentary suspect.

I got to ask a doctor more about that sort of lifestyle at dinner. Rip and I had been invited to a small gathering at the home of a Bryn Derwyn board member, Ronald Moats. His wife, Penny, was inclined to embrace dramatic fads, and I looked forward to the exposure as one looks forward to a foreign vacation.

Penny did not disappoint. This year's living room featured Danish Modern revival with accents of the greener earth tones. Texture assaulted the senses, from satiny wood to burlap that could file your nails. Three striped sofas encircled a driftwood-and-glass coffee table. Most of us stood, clutching hard at our sangria so as not to spill.

"What's this?" asked a woman named Glo, whom I had just met. She referred to an hors d'oeuvre our hostess was huckstering.

"Pot sticker," Penny replied. She wore close-fitting black with a macrame necklace of dangling buttons. The shocking red of both her lipstick and manicure matched the brightest of the buttons.

Glo speared a miniature stuffed dumpling with a toothpick and queried, "Low fat?"

"No fat," came the defensive answer. Whether or not it was true, it was the only possible response.

Tall and full-breasted, with severe black hair and salon-style makeup, I suspected Glo of concealing an imperfection under her long chiffon skirt. "Did you hear what they're doing in Japan?" she addressed me.

"About what?" I asked, but another voice over my shoulder laughed, "The surgical tape?"

Glo and the giggler, a short, chunky honey-blonde named Sue, vented their amusement over whatever the Japanese were currently doing with the tape.

I had to ask.

"Oh, dear. You didn't see *Newsweek*? They're wrapping it around their fingers to lose weight."

"I hear there's a new pill coming out," Glo prompted. "Not addictive, makes you feel full, and no serious physical, side effects."

"Just constipation or diarrhea. Or else it makes you pee all the time."

"My sister's church is pushing a faith healing thing. You sort of pray the weight away..."

"What about that leptin they discovered?"

"They know about it; they just don't know what to do with it."

Glo and her compatriot, Sue, went on to laugh and lament over the many diet fads they'd tried over the years. "The Grapefruit Diet."

"The Drinking Man's Diet."

"The Pasta Diet."

"The Protein Diet?" I offered, and both turned to stare. "The what?" They were interested. I was speaking their language.

"Karl Vogel, the nutritionist who died this week, sometimes prescribed a protein diet. Know anything about it?"

A fourth woman joined us. "It's reminiscent of the sixties trend started by Stillman, Atkins, and Tamower.

Downplays carbohydrates–pasta, potatoes, bagels, rice cakes–in favor of meat, tofu, eggs, cheese, bacon, even pork rinds."

"Does it work?" I asked.

The newcomer shrugged and smiled. "We've got an epidemic of obesity in the United States–about seventy-five percent of us over the age of twenty-five are overweight As a result, we spend seventy billion dollars a year on related health problems. If somebody had the definitive answer, we'd all be thin."

"You're a doctor," I observed. A doctor talking about weight loss–for free. Glo and Sue watched her lips like cats salivating over cream.

"Pam Renke," the woman admitted, extending her hand. "Ginger Struve Barnes," I replied.

"How are you familiar with Karl Vogel's work?" she asked. "Surely you weren't a client."

The cats turned to slink away. Pam Renke touched one of their arms. "Eat sensibly and exercise," she advised. "No extremes."

Disappointed, the two women eased their way toward the bar, and Pam turned back with a philosophical smile. "Vogel?" she prompted me.

"I'm a friend of his ex-wife," I replied. "I've been speaking to some of his clients because of his death."

Pam raised an unkempt eyebrow. Actually, in contrast to Glo and Sue her whole appearance seemed oblivious to style. My attention took in only her hazel eyes and the quick mind behind them. No doubt Penny Moats was conducting another of her mix-and-match dinners.

"You're an investigator?"

That flustered me, and I must have blushed. "A well-intentioned friend," I hastened to explain. "I'm trying to help Linda keep her dog. It's a long story."

"I'm not going anywhere."

I admitted I would be grateful for her impressions. Sometimes restating the facts to an unbiased listener revealed the flaws in my own thinking.

Pam smiled and gestured toward the sofa. "Glad to try." I joined her down on those low cushions. After sketching in the basics, I began to describe Debbie Greene's home life.

Pam nodded knowingly. "Early puberty, heavy family responsibilities, perfectionist personality—anorexia nervosa."

"Was it Karl's fault?"

"No, but don't try to tell that to the father."

"How about Karl's diet failures? I was told two women, Annie Snellenberg and Darlene Polk, hated him enough to kill him. Could one of them have retrained his dog?"

"Why not? Being obese doesn't exempt anybody from strong emotions."

Which, of course, reminded me of Nancy Carlino's vehement opinions.

The doctor tilted her head and finished her thought. "Just think how passive-aggressives manage to get what they want."

I laughed. "By remote control?"

Pam snickered just to be sociable, but she had intended her message to be a serious one.

She was right, of course. With enough compulsion most anyone can, and will, orchestrate quite a bit of damage—no matter what difficulties stood in the way.

The thought ruined what was left of my appetite.

Chapter 17

INSIDE THE AIRPORT garage at about ten o'clock on Sunday morning, the last day of June, I stopped the Subaru in front of a white sawhorse barring me from where I wanted to go. Dr. Fleming was retired; I thought he might be elderly enough to appreciate a short walk from the terminal to the car.

I shrugged to myself and drove around the barrier. As if I'd conjured it up, there was an empty slot right next to the door. Maybe this morning wouldn't be as bad as I had imagined.

Some of the passengers exiting the jetway of Dr. Fleming's gate blinked at the fluorescent lights and squinted to find their greeters. Looking bored, others simply moved off toward the luggage claim. I held an old shirt cardboard that said Dr. Fleming, but so far none of the elderly men who disembarked gave me more than a passing glance.

Finally, a man emerged wearing a rumpled, madras sport coat and carrying a two-handled navy-blue gym bag. His khakis revealed a little extra ankle as if they'd been thrown in the dryer on high. His white oxford shirt would never need ironing and might not even biodegrade.

The man gave the female flight attendant who followed him a peck on the cheek and an exceedingly wide smile as if she had done him some extraordinary service. The young woman beamed as if he had done the same for her.

"Oh, excuse me," Dr. Fleming said as he approached. "Sorry to make you wait, but I had to thank Michelle. I don't like to fly."

"And?"

"She fixed me a drink...warm milk," he added to accommodate my questioning expression. "So, you're the brilliant Ginny Barnes."

"Gin, or Ginger, please."

"Right, right," he said seeming to appreciate the subtle difference. "Call me Doc. Mathias sounds like an old man."

"Welcome to Philadelphia," I said, extending my hand. I had already stashed the shirtboard in a trashcan.

Fleming's face lifted into a wedge of wrinkles like the popcorn patriarch Orville Redenbacher or perhaps a Caucasian ET. He wore black-rimmed trifocals and possessed a shock of white wavy hair many women would have envied. The teeth contained inside an unusually large mouth were obviously his own. I estimated his age at somewhere between sixty and ninety.

We set off down the pier at a brisk clip. He was tall, perhaps 6'3", and stoop-shouldered, but definitely not lame. "You're the reason I was asked to come, aren't you. Gin Barnes?" He said, glancing back to find me trotting to keep up.

I mumbled something about Timothy Bedoes.

"Aw, nonsense, girl. Timmy told me it was your idea. Brilliant. Absolutely brilliant. Know your dogs, do you?" As we reached the long, nearly empty ramp leading to the garage, I thought about how Gretsky had awakened me again at six a.m., about how horribly behaved he was in general. "Not really."

"But you must. Not too many people know dogs sometimes try to revive their deceased masters."

I stopped short. "What?"

Mathias Reining stared at me, thoroughly perplexed. "Wasn't that what you thought?"

I gulped, trying to erase the image of an anguished Tibor trying to revive Karl.

Animals comprehended death, that much I knew. Our

veterinarian once explained how they benefit from viewing the finality of a companion's demise for themselves, much in the way we do, as if by confronting death an instinctive need is met. Deprived of that opportunity, a pet might feel unjustly abandoned and the mourning period would be prolonged.

And yet...could animals really mourn as deeply as this man, this forensic pathologist, suggested?

Something I'd once seen years before came vividly into focus: twilight. The four of us Barneses were walking up to Rip's mother's front door when a squirrel carrying another, obviously dead, squirrel in its mouth came within four feet of us. The sorrow in the surviving mate's eyes was impossible to forget.

Yet there had been more than pain in those eyes. He, or she, seemed to beg us for help.

"That wasn't what you thought?" Mathias Fleming queried again.

Had it been, maybe subconsciously? Who knew?

I wagged my head no.

Fleming raised a bony finger. "Our secret" He turned to continue his Ichabod Crane lope down the corridor.

"Is something like that really possible?" I asked.

Fleming stopped and whirled. "That's it. In a nutshell."

"What's it?" Was I always going to have trouble catching up to this man?

The finger raised again. "Reasonable doubt."

At last I saw. Just the fact that animals sometimes tried to revive their deceased loved ones suggested Tibor's bite might not have been the cause of Karl's death. He just might have left his tooth marks and bloodied himself *after* Karl died in a desperate, instinctive, and foolishly futile attempt to help. That in turn opened up the investigation to many other possibilities not yet explored. The whole idea stunned me.

"You coming?" Dr. Fleming–Doc–asked, hands and gym bag on hip.

The rest of the walk to my car was accomplished without conversation, except for a negative reply when I asked about more luggage.

Bristling with eagerness, Fleming proclaimed the day "Exciting" to the world in general, adding a hearty, "I love this business," as he folded himself into the Subaru.

The morgue was set perhaps a block off the Schuylkill Expressway across from a hospital in the vicinity of the University of Pennsylvania. I had driven by it a dozen times on the way to baseball or football games and even the Philadelphia Flower Show back when that event was held at the old Civic Center. I hadn't once noticed the morgue.

Leaving my car next to the few others in the large lot, I followed Doc to the doorway, expecting to shake hands and part company. Before I could ask whether he had a ride to wherever he was staying, he spoke into the intercom by the doorjamb. "Dr. Fleming and Ms. Barnes," he announced to the person inside.

"Be right up," came the answer.

"I thought I was leaving," I said.

"Oh," he said, surprised. "You're not taking me to my son's?"

Timothy Bedoes, manipulating me again.

"You don't have another ride?"

Doc's silence told me all I needed to know. "I'm sorry," he said. "I, too, made an assumption. Since it was your idea, I thought you'd like to be on hand when I find out whether Tibor was the killer. But since..." His voice trailed off, perhaps remembering I hadn't been nearly as smart as he had assumed. Young Ginger had disappointed granddad with a stupid chess move, and suddenly the promise he thought he'd perceived had been reduced to beginner's luck. I wanted to regain this man's esteem, for real this time.

"I *am* interested…"

"Great. That's great. We could use another witness."

My stomach flew into a panic. An autopsy. I had just agreed to watch an autopsy. What were you thinking, Gin? Exactly what were you thinking?

A tall, fortyish blond man in a white lab coat personally opened the door for us. Since it was Sunday morning, I supposed work was confined to oddities such as Dr. Fleming's visit.

We were led through a spacious reception area with lots of soft sofas and chairs for waiting. The corridors began to confuse me, but soon enough we emerged into an antiseptic-looking room of stainless-steel tables and spotless tile flooring. It might have been a mass-production-style surgi-center with perhaps a dozen or more stations lined up against two sides of the lengthy room. Except surgi-centers didn't need those glowing purple bug lights.

Mercifully, no other cadavers but Karl's were anywhere in sight.

I can't say he looked serene. He looked horrible, of course, and my stomach twisted and my head reeled. Yet everybody else was behaving like a professional, so I kept quiet and stood still until I could see the situation as they saw it.

A plain-clothes police officer there to observe shook hands and introduced himself as Detective Craig Mansfield. Our escort, the pathologist who had done the preliminary examination, was a man named Dr. Charles Shields. Fleming insisted on calling him Chuck. The cop seemed intent upon his chewing gum and his camera. All the friendly chitchat was left to Doc.

Me, I kept busy making my mental escape. For example, I spent considerable time trying to remember the words to Kermit the Frog's song, "It Ain't Easy Being Green."

Karl had been washed and covered with a clean sheet that only exposed what Fleming needed to see while he needed to see it. Once, the sheet rode up, and I was confronted with a pair of pale, no-longer-functional feet. The toe-tag rumors you heard were true.

At one point Doc grasped my biceps in his bony hands and physically positioned me so I could see better. "Can't be much of a witness hiding behind that post," he scolded kindly.

I gulped.

The part I watched seemed to take forever. Doc mixed a big batch of tan plastery stuff, then applied it to Karl's wounds with what looked like a large wooden tongue depressor. When the stuff set, it became a flexible, almost rubbery replica of the bites, revealing the size and shape of the dog's teeth.

Along with an overall numbness, I became quite twitchy anticipating the results. Meanwhile, Doc hummed and smiled to himself as if he really did love his work: Combined with the borrowed lab coat and concealing rubber gloves, he looked quite young. To see his face, you'd have thought he was cooking up filets on his barbecue grill.

Ugh. The image of meat was a bad one. I couldn't help thinking of Karl on that grill. I swayed. The doctor named Chuck brought me a chair.

"Thanks," I said weakly. "We almost done?"

"Yup," Doc said gleefully. "No doubt about it. Two different dogs."

Chuck huffed. The cop snorted, and I leaped out of the chair.

"Two? You're sure?" We all jabbered at once.

"Com'ere, Chuck. I'll show you," Doc said politely. The other man's abbreviated preliminary examination was the reason the discrepancies hadn't shown up before. Also, to be fair, Shields had agreed to wait for Bedoes's dog-bite expert to complete the autopsy.

With the mold in his left hand Doc held a ruler against what were clearly three separate sets of upper and lower canine teeth. One set was noticeably wider spaced. The other two matched each other. Of those that matched, the Upper left canine tooth appeared to be shorter.

I asked why, and Doc's face glowed. The granddaughter might have the real stuff after all. "Because, my dear, this dog had a broken upper left canine."

Detective Mansfield abruptly excused himself to make a cellular phone call over in the corner.

"Will you be able to identify the dog from the bites?" I asked Fleming.

"The breed?" he suggested. "Only in general terms, but off the record it looks right for a pit bull to me. Now you bring me the right dog, we do another mold...then I can testify it's the one. Until then ..." He shook his head.

"Amazing," Chuck said, raking his slender hand through his hair. "I don't know how I missed that."

"Because you don't think like this young lady here. You figure the dog was caught with blood on his mouth, it's the only dog around–that's the dog. So, you save a few bucks on casting material and help the prosecutor prove what he already knows."

"But..." Chuck wore his embarrassment like a bad sunburn.

Doc placed a comforting hand on his arm. "So next time you spend the few bucks and do the castings. We got it right now. Settle back down, folks. I'm not finished."

He whipped the sheet off Karl's torso, revealing an assortment of long frantic scratches.

When I thought I saw Doc reaching for a knife, I excused myself. An hour later, resembling the cat who ate the canary, he collected me from the reception area.

"Well?" I prompted.

"Missing right front claw, too," he announced with a broad smile.

Tibor was an exemplary specimen of a German shepherd with teeth and claws intact. He had not killed Karl.

I whistled through my teeth.

Chapter 18

DOC FLEMING'S bachelor son lived in a storybook stone gatehouse by a pond outside of Wayne. He happened to be a pediatric podiatrist and was on duty all weekend, another reason my taxi services had been requested.

I hopped out of the car to be certain my new acquaintance could get inside; and after he successfully unlocked the door, we stood a moment smiling at each other.

"I'll tell Timmy," he said, referring to Timothy Bedoes, the attorney who had summoned him. "You want to tell his client?"

"Thanks, I'd really love to."

We grinned a little more.

"See ya," I said, feeling at least as smitten as the flight attendant Doc had befriended so quickly.

"Bye," he said.

This time I wasn't going to Linda's at noon without my own lunch. Since I couldn't think of a deli that would be open, I stopped at the food court of Genuardi's market and came away with a couple of chicken-salad sandwiches and two cans of Diet Sprite.

Linda greeted me in her bathrobe and slippers, a mug of coffee in her hand. She wore no makeup and her curly hair suggested the shape of a partially deflated soccer ball. Dark circles under her eyes weighed down her face, and my perkiness seemed to bother her like sunglare. The word "hangover" came to mind.

I told her, "This is the last time I'll drop in, I promise. But I've got really great news."

She needed the news before she would consider a smile, but she stepped back from the door.

"Tibor didn't do it," I said.

"Wha–?" Linda's arms circled back and sloshed coffee on the door and the hardwood floor. She set the mug on a bookshelf and tugged at my arm until she could force me into the nearest living-room chair. Then she sat knee-to-knee with me on the adjacent sofa.

"What do you mean, Tibor didn't do it?"

I explained about Mathias Fleming and the castings he took of the dog bites, how the measurements and broken tooth showed a second dog was involved. "Also, the dog that killed Karl had a missing claw."

Linda clasped me with her fingers and grinned into my face. Tears glittered in her eyes. Then she let go and flopped back against the sofa cushions. "Amazing. Absolutely amazing." She wiped her eyes with a fuzzy yellow sleeve. "Did you call the SPCA yet? They'll have to return Tibor to me now, won't they?"

I had been too busy being shocked and delighted to be quite that practical; but at Linda's urging, I placed the call. She hovered in the kitchen doorway while I spoke to a caretaker.

"Nobody with any authority is there on Sundays," I explained when I got off the phone. "I'll call again tomorrow."

"Let's celebrate," Linda suggested. "Gin and tonic okay?"

"I'll stick with Diet Sprite, but you go ahead."

A couple minutes later we were sitting on the floor on either side of her mahogany coffee table eating chicken salad, sipping our beverages, and giggling like a couple of teenagers having a pajama party.

Then suddenly Linda's expression changed. She stared at an envelope lying on the coffee table as if it were capable of convicting her. I noticed there was no return address.

"What?" I asked with dismay.

"Nothing," she said with a wave of her hand, but her eyes strayed back to the letter. I couldn't help remembering the one she wrote Karl, the one that had caused her to be arrested.

"Are you superstitious?" she asked.

I shrugged. "Maybe a little," I answered truthfully.

"Well, I just got one of those religious chain letters promising great luck if I send it to twelve of my friends and disasters beyond description if I don't."

"That's what this is?" I picked up the envelope and glanced at the letter inside. It was indeed one of those lengthy epistles promising wealth and happiness if the recipient sent it on, and miserable luck if she didn't.

Linda shivered just watching me read it, but perhaps she could envision a horrible fate all too easily after the night she spent in prison.

I brightened my voice. "Why not do what I do?" I suggested. "Photocopy the thing. Then pick a street where you don't know anybody and the mailboxes are down by the road."

Linda eyed me sideways.

"Then you drive along and deliver a big batch of good luck to every mailbox until you run out of letters."

"That's the stupidest thing I ever heard," Linda snorted.

"Suit yourself," I waffled, embarrassed now that I had confessed to such a silly solution.

"A *wonderful* stupid thing," Linda amended. "You're so...so upbeat about everything. Even when I..." she looked at me with embarrassment now, remembering how she had treated me in high school. "I'm so sorry, Gin. I was always mean to you, and you just...you just took it. I really missed out, didn't I?"

"On me? No." I tucked down my chin, shook my head. "I was clueless. We never would have become friends back then. That was just wishful thinking on my part."

Linda reached out and tapped the back of my hand. "We're doing better now, aren't we? It's the one good thing that's come out of this mess." Her soft expression edged precariously close to becoming maudlin, so I braced myself for a dose of overblown sentiment.

Actually, what she said wasn't so bad. In fact, it was quite nice. Linda lifted her eyes to mine and said, "If there's anything I can ever do for you..."

Which was the opening I needed.

"Well," I began, in an effort to lighten things up. "There is one thing." Taking my time, I described Gretsky's extensive efforts to control his universe.

When I was done, Linda simply said, "Dominance down."

"What's that?" I asked, wiping mayonnaise from my lip with a napkin to hide my disappointment. Weeks of dog-training hell couldn't possibly be boiled down to two words. Could they?

"It's how mother dogs teach their puppies who's who."

"Oh, please, please, please show me how to do it. That dog's driving me crazy."

Linda disentangled her bare legs from under the coffee table until she was kneeling on the carpet with open space in front of her.

"You get the dog to lie down, either with the down command or force."

Gretsky would usually sit for me if he wasn't too wound up, and from there I knew how to press my fingers on either side of the base of his neck to get him to lie down. If he was already too overwrought, I was hard-pressed to get him to do anything. "Force?" I asked.

"Wrestle him to the ground."

"I guess I could manage that."

"Then, with his back toward your lap, you hold his bottom legs with your hands, making sure one elbow is jammed up under his chin and the other is resting on his hip. The idea is to immobilize him so he can't roll over or get away."

"This works?"

"Um-humm. Keep him like that for twenty minutes the first time. Later you may only need five minutes. He'll settle down because he has no choice, and he'll also understand who's the boss."

The overjoyed part of me wanted to embrace Linda for the mere possibility of getting somewhere with our four-legged brat.

My skeptical part wanted it in writing.

THE BARNESES' favorite summer Sunday meal was London broil on the grill, potatoes in foil roasted on the grill, fresh bread, and salad.

Gretsky decided to pitch a fit just as we served it up and were headed for the patio with our plates. Barking, whirling, poking, grumbling in his throat–he wanted something. Not food. Not exercise, for he and Garry had run around the yard all afternoon. Not anything any of us could name. He seemed to be having the temper tantrum of an overextended child.

I handed Rip my plate, said I'd be out in twenty minutes, and told everybody, "Go ahead and eat without me."

As soon as the patio screen closed, Gretsky came over to investigate and mutter. He was down and dominated before he knew what hit him. He squiggled and squirmed and glared until the whites of his eyes showed. In about five minutes he sighed and relaxed. In another ten minutes he was asleep.

My cold London broil never tasted so good.

FIRST THING Monday morning I phoned Alice, my contact at the PSPCA and explained as best I could about Tibor's innocence. She received the part about Tibor biting Karl out of distress without undue surprise, probably because she'd heard of similar incidents. Yet her enthusiasm remained guarded.

"That's really good news for your friend," she concluded, "and for Tibor..."

I finished the sentence for her. "...but it's still up to the judge."

"Yes," she agreed gratefully. I could almost see the tilt of her eyebrows, the wrinkles on her brow. She must have thought I hoped to pick Tibor up immediately, so I assured her Linda and I understood she needed to follow procedure.

She gave me the name of the judge to pass on to Timothy Bedoes, who would be able to deliver the new evidence in the proper form.

Like the polite person I am, I thanked the woman. Then I placed a call to Linda's lawyer.

"Good morning," he said soberly.

Again, much less enthusiasm than I expected. What was wrong with these people?

Perhaps Bedoes thought I was someone else. "It's me, Gin Barnes. Linda's friend," I said, hoping to bring him around.

"Yes, I know," he replied, his answer followed by an ominous pause.

"You were right about. Dr. Fleming. He's terrific. Did he call you?" Maybe the attorney had been unavailable when Doc tried to reach him. Maybe he had not yet heard about the second dog.

"Yes. We spoke."

But...

"What's wrong?" I asked.

"The police have a witness who saw Linda's car near the scene of the crime. I'm afraid they have impressions of both her footprints and her tire tracks."

I sat down heavily on Chelsea's hairbrush.

"Ouch," I said.

I might have said more, but that about summed it up.

Chapter 19

LINDA WORE A sleeveless, pearl-gray linen outfit and matching high-heeled sandals; I wore the plaid walking shorts and navy T-shirt with Keds I'd chosen that morning thinking I had dressed for any eventuality. Meeting with Linda and her attorney had not figured into my calculations.

"Were you there?" Bedoes asked his client with arms folded sternly across his chest. Shirtsleeves rolled as usual, he leaned semi-casually against the front of his large desk. Linda paced around behind the two clients' chairs. From the chair on the right, I had to twist to watch the drama unfolding beside and behind me.

"No." Linda wrapped her arms across herself also, but tightly, as if holding in some guilty information.

"Then how do you explain your tire tracks–and quite probably your footprints–in the dirt under that tree?" Sharing information as required by law, the police had alerted the defense attorney to the nature of the new evidence.

Apparently, Detective Mansfield, the Philadelphia cop in charge of Karl's case, had been sharper than his gum-chewing, lackadaisical manner suggested. At the time of the autopsy he happened to be missing his own religious service; so when he saw the case against Linda slipping, he put two and two together and remembered the Methodist church located little more than a block from the crime scene. From its parking lot a person might have sneaked undetected through the few woodsy back yards to observe Karl's early morning training sessions.

When he had called in the new development from the morgue, Mansfield requested that someone question the minister of the Methodist church.

And that person found out that yes, the rectory was adjacent to the church; and yes, one day in the beginning of the week the reverend had seen a car parked just off the church lot. The sun had been up just enough for him to notice the color and make, a dark-blue Lincoln, which he remembered because he admired the car and wished he might one day own one. Also, it had been secluded off the macadam, next to a yew and shaded by a very bushy maple, odd because there was so much space available in the regular lot.

Which day? "Monday or Tuesday." He could not be more specific. His routine was to rise at dawn and have coffee before getting dressed. Most days were the same in that respect, and unless the weather was severe, which it had not been, one weekday seemed like the next.

What did he think at the time? "That someone was having a romantic tryst with one of the neighbors and didn't want his or her car seen."

Bedoes had related all this to us when Linda arrived at his office. I got there first, but then I hadn't bothered to change my clothes. Linda, apparently, had been in less of a rush.

Now she bit her lip and turned away from her questioner. Even in profile, the indecision on her face was plain.

Finally, she sighed and said, "Is what I say still confidential with her here?"

Bedoes sighed too, perhaps with disgust. "Look. We've got the second dog now, which opens up all sorts of possibilities. You're not out of the woods on that, since you're as capable of training another dog as you are Tibor. But if you've got any explanation at all for the tire tracks, you might as well tell it. It can't be worse than the police version, and it might be better."

"Okay." Linda wrung her fists and paced some more.

She looked inward rather than at either her lawyer or me.

"I was there," she said.

I couldn't help it, I made a sound. A gasp or a groan, it didn't matter. Both Linda and Bedoes glared at me.

"Go on," Bedoes prompted.

"Monday morning. Not Tuesday." She watched me to make sure I didn't argue or interrupt.

"Why?" Bedoes asked quietly.

Linda threw out her hands. "I was spying on Karl. He's dating someone, was dating someone. I figured if she stayed overnight, I'd see her leave for work. I was jealous– okay?"

"You still loved him?" I was more surprised by that admission than the fact that her car had been seen.

"Yes!" Linda hurled the word belligerently.

After a quick mental run-through of her and Karl's history–from the volatile marriage to the vituperative divorce–I decided to believe her. Just because Rip and I had so far enjoyed a relatively placid relationship didn't mean I couldn't become just as embittered as Linda if he betrayed me. In fact I might become bitter *because* I still loved the guy.

"Was that the only time you spied on Karl?"

Linda shook her head. "I went a few other times, but I parked different places."

Bedoes pinched his lip between his fingers and stared at the floor. "When was the last time it rained?"

We put our heads together and came up with the previous Sunday night, seven days before, further support for Linda's claim of being there Monday morning. The soil would have been soft enough to take clear impressions, and the intervening good weather would have preserved them.

"Might help," Bedoes mused. "But let's go back to your feelings for Karl. Can anyone else swear you still cared for him? A friend or relative you might have confided in?"

Linda came up dry on that one but promised to give it some thought.

Bedoes talked around the new problems a while longer. Then he finally patted Linda's shoulder and said, "Try not to worry. We'll get a handle on this. Darkest before dawn, and all that."

Linda dismissed Bedoes's words with a scowl.

I left feeling responsible for making them come true. With the authorities still so focused on Linda, I didn't trust them to recognize evidence of her innocence if they tripped over it.

Bedoes was right, I cared more than the police did.

Dr. Fleming was also right. My view of the problem was that of the bystander looking over the shoulder of the computer geek. While the geek thought, "If I push button A, B should happen," I was wondering about the little message down there in the corner.

At the moment, I needed to talk out the second-dog development until I got a sense of direction. Rip would have been my first choice of confidant; but in addition to the ongoing gym construction, I knew he had a day full of meetings on next year's curriculum, scheduling, the student handbook, and a particularly long one regarding Bryn Derwyn's budget. Also, he probably knew less than I did about dogs.

Dr. Fleming, on the other hand, knew plenty. And as a bonus, he was already familiar with Linda's case. When I called from the receptionist's phone in Bedoes's office, he assured me he had been doing nothing more important than reading; and I was most welcome to stop by.

When I arrived at his son's house, Doc led me through an iron gate under an archway dripping with wisteria into a shaded outdoor room enclosed on three sides with greenery. More wisteria covered some lattice overhead. Ornamental ivy on white trellises formed cool shady walls, and lush moss grew between the rounds of sawed tree trunks used to form the patio floor.

The padded wrought-iron furniture proved to be much more comfortable than expected, and a pitcher of spiced grape juice and glasses of ice waited on a small circular glass-topped table next to the book Doc had been reading.

"I should probably shop or do the Barnes museum or at least the Farmers' Market while I'm here," Doc apologized. "But when Toby's working, I admit I prefer the quiet of his little patio. Any relation?"

"Pardon me?"

"Barnes."

"Oh, no. And I don't blame you. This is exquisite." Lining the path to the pond twenty feet away were clumps of interesting grasses and flowers. Past the pond, complete with squawking ducks, spread a vista of trees and lawn leading to a picturesque white mansion well past yelling distance. "If I had a spot like this, I wouldn't budge either."

Fleming smiled. "Sure you would." I caught him gauging the expression in my eyes, so I let him see that he was right. After a couple of hours, I probably *would* leap out of my seat and start to weed.

"So where do these new tire tracks leave you?" he asked. He wore white slacks, loafers with no socks, and a pink, blue, and yellow plaid shirt. Apparently, the Fleming men refused to be threatened by pastels. "Back at the pit bull, I'm afraid."

Fleming nodded. "It could have been another breed, of course."

"But you don't think so."

"If I were going to train a dog to kill, that would be my choice." He poured us some juice almost too pretty to drink.

"Trouble is I can't imagine any of my suspects housing a pit bull, training it, transporting it. One of the women can scarcely walk."

"Somebody did it."

"I wonder where you get yourself a pit bull."

Doc shrugged, sipped his drink.

"I'll ask at Braxton's." My favorite pet supply store. "Gretsky needs another collar anyway." Growing boy.

Now I felt buoyant, as if my objective had been met. Just as Braxton's had once given me a printout of Irish setter breeders, they would do the same for pit bulls. The list would be short. After a few visits, one of the breeders would remember selling a dog to one of the suspects...

"Phillies play tonight?" Doc asked.

"No. They're off." We went off in that direction and a few others, until it was time for me to leave.

"Keep me posted," Doc requested, and I believed he meant it.

I was happy to agree. He was a very nice, very interesting man. And considering his age, Rip probably wouldn't even raise an eyebrow over our friendship.

"Is Toby by any chance short for Tobias?" I asked at the iron gate. Mathias/Tobias; father/son.

"No, Tobin. Why do you ask?"

"Bad guess." And just when I was feeling like such an ace detective.

Chapter 20

THERE WAS JUST enough time left to pick up Gretsky and get to Braxton's Animal Works before it closed.

The store was on Lancaster, one building off Sugartown Road. As usual, hay bales and a metal cage of colorful rubber balls were displayed outside the entrance.

Since I needed a lull in the pet shop trade to ask my offbeat questions, I was pleased to notice that at that time of day most people were shopping at the produce stand that faced Lancaster.

The tall helper with long, medium-brown hair led Gretsky and me past the bulletin board, the dog biscuit shelf, the book room, the bin of rawhide bones (seconds), and the wall of toys, to the ten-foot-long freestanding wall hung with collars and leashes. The Great One nodded and nosed everything on the way by, waving his fringed tail like royalty bestowing favor on his realm. The salesman fitted him for a blue, sixteen-inch nylon choke collar before I dared to broach my question.

"Do you by any chance know where someone would acquire a pit bull?"

The young man stood to escape Gretsky's friendly tongue and blinked. "A pit bull?" He glanced down at my Irish setter and seemed to wonder why I would also want a pit bull. Certainly not as a companion.

Since the truth would have taken us past closing time, a lie seemed expedient.

"A friend of mine wants a guard dog, and an old neighbor who moved away had a very sweet-natured pit bull. I'm trying to remember the breeder who sold my neighbor his, so my friend can get one from there."

"Oh. Well, pit bulls are a mixed breed–did you know that? But the mix is now a recognized breed, the

American pit bull terrier. There's also the American Staffordshire terrier, and the bull terrier. They're all mastiff types. Various coloration, but otherwise they look pretty similar."

I agreed. The ones caged at the PSPCA had each looked like a pug-nosed fireplug covered with muscle.

"Can you give me a list of breeders?"

"No."

"No?"

"There aren't any around here."

"There aren't?" I chewed my lip, again thinking of the row of bite cases housed with Tibor. How could there be so many pit bulls if no breeders existed? Should I perhaps be looking for a doggie dating service?

"So where do the criminals get theirs?" I asked.

"Anywhere they can," the tall guy suggested.

Underground. From private individuals who did not advertise they raised pit bulls.

It figured.

Preoccupied with that thought my attention may have strayed from Gretsky while we waited our turn at the cash register. And maybe that was why our darling pet chose to remind me of his presence, although he may have had another reason altogether. Anyway, he lifted his leg on a corner display.

Face flaming, I swatted his flank and rushed him out to the car.

Then, forced to return in ignominy, I imagined myself invisible while dabbing at the offending drips with a couple of tissues from my purse. Was that...? Yes, one box had apparently been hit. I cleaned it off, then grabbed it.

The tall guy waited with a wastebasket, but I was too embarrassed to thank him.

"I'll take these, too," I said instead, handing him the

box to go with the collar.

Which was how I ended up spending five ninety-nine for a package of "Dog-Repellant Trash Bags" I already knew didn't work.

Before leaving the parking lot, I selected some magnificent early tomatoes from the produce stand and some corn that must have been hustled from its far-away field to Devon quick before the silk dried; so far Pennsylvania corn only reached knee-high, and the price of the corn I bought seemed to include first-class airfare for each ear.

The delay did little toward rubbing Gretsky's nose in his faux pas; he had gone to sleep in the back seat. I, at least, felt less like I was being run out of town, and now I had something to go with the leftover London broil sandwiches I planned for dinner.

When we got home, my driveway was graced by a blue Volkswagen Fox sporting a bumper sticker that read, "Meat is Murder."

"Oh, hi, Mrs. Barnes," Stevie Luckenbill greeted me at my own front door. Over a pale yellow T-shirt she wore threadbare denim overalls that were maybe boys' size medium, and widely strapped sandals in either girls' size large or a ladies' size three. From the day's heat, her hair lay in feathery clumps.

"Your husband's meeting was running late, so I brought the kids home. Then I didn't want to leave them by themselves..." She flipped a hand.

"I told her we'd be fine," Chelsea piped up behind the young woman. At only thirteen our daughter was already taller than Stevie. Garry, too.

A blond elf. Stevie Luckenbill looked like a blond elf.

"Thank you very much, Stevie," I said sincerely as I maneuvered past everybody into the kitchen with my bags of produce. "Would you like to stay for dinner?"

"What are you having?" Her face crinkled around those intense blue eyes as she peeked into the bags.

"Corn, tomatoes, and," I winced as I said it, "London broil sandwiches."

Stevie flicked her finger against the bags with a pop. "Did you know forty percent of all Central American rainforests were destroyed to create pasture for beef cattle?"

"Really?"

"Yes, and just one wildlife reserve in Costa Rica contains more bird species than you'll find on the entire North American continent?"

"Ummm."

"Oh, yes. Half of all the species in the world inhabit the three point four million-square-mile green band that encircles the equator."

"How about dinner, Stevie? Can you stay?"

"No. My boyfriend's expecting me. But thanks." She glanced at the microwave clock, gasped, and hustled toward the front door. "Bye, kids," she shouted.

"Another time," I suggested, "and thanks again for bringing Chelsea and Garry home." I had to raise my voice to be heard halfway down the front walk.

"No problem," Stevie shouted back with a wave.

Phew. That girl was exhausting. Then I remembered today's field trip.

"How was the zoo?" I asked Garry, who stood at the door watching Stevie speed away. He shrugged and replied, "Okay, I guess." Then he sauntered down the hall toward the TV room.

"Chelsea?" I asked. She seemed to be examining the tomatoes I bought one by one.

"Sad," she said.

My eyes widened. Usually the zoo was the campers' second-favorite outing, runner-up only to Goodwin's

Dairy Farm where they sold ice cream.

How so?" I asked.

"Tigers pacing, cheetahs wagging their heads. They're like all nuts from incarceration, Mom. It's really terrible."

Maybe they were, maybe they weren't. I reserved judgment. "Did the little kids have a good time?" I asked, hoping against hope.

Chelsea shrugged. "I guess so." She wandered away, leaving the tomatoes free to roll around–or off–the counter according to the dictates of gravity. I spent a few minutes slicing two, preparing the corn to be zapped in the microwave, and assembling the sandwiches. I was just setting the table when Rip arrived home.

After we kissed hello and determined that all the major things in our lives remained stable, I put my question to him. "Any feedback on the zoo?"

"Ugh, the zoo," he replied. "Amanda Carling came back in tears, Gin."

"The six-year-old, looks like Shirley Temple?"

"That's the one. I took her aside to ask what was wrong, and you know what she said?"

"When she stopped sobbing?"

"Right. 'They should let all the animals go. It isn't fair.'" He said that imitating the voice of Amanda Carling as best he could. "Guess I'll be getting a call from her parents."

More than a few calls was my bet. Poor Rip. "Toilet-flushing problem solved?"

"I hope so. I spoke to Stevie, and she seemed to understand. Of course, the kids were out most of the day. We'll see what happens tomorrow."

Garry heard the click of a dinner platter touching the table and materialized. "Which club do you think I should join, Dad?" he asked as he took his seat. "Dolphins or beavers?"

He had changed into a white tank top, a.k.a "muscle shirt," presumably to give his lanky body incentive.

"What do you mean, club?" Rip asked. "What's that all about?" Chelsea had also appeared and settled into her chair with a flourish.

"We're all joining organizations, Dad," Garry answered.

"Who's involved?"

"All the camp kids," our daughter joined in. "Stevie handed out lists on the bus this morning so we could check out the endangered animals and make better-informed choices. I picked bats," she announced importantly. "They're really amazing. Did you know the twenty million Mexican free-tail bats that live in Bracken Cave eat two hundred and fifty tons of insects every night?"

Garry, our resident skeptic, snorted his opinion of her statistic, and Chelsea shot him a withering glance.

"Also, they don't really get tangled in your hair or transmit disease like most people think. The world would really be in bad shape without them."

"Is that so?" Rip remarked.

"Yes, that's so," Chelsea asserted. "So, I'm joining Bat Conservation International–if it's okay with you guys."

"Sure," I mumbled over a mouthful of my London broil and tomato sandwich. It didn't taste nearly as good as I had hoped.

"I can't decide between dolphins and beavers," Garry repeated. "Dolphins are really smart and all, but too many kids like dolphins. I kind of think I like beavers better." Rip's face screwed up into a strange expression. His eyes sparkled and his lips twitched in and out of a lopsided grin. He appeared to be considering a lewd remark.

"Robert Ripley Barnes," I warned. "Don't you dare say what you're thinking."

Chapter 21

TUESDAY MORNING, July 2, the children departed with their father to go to camp. In among the swimsuits and sandwiches in their backpacks were checks and stamped envelopes that would surely go far toward saving the world, at least as far as bats and beavers were concerned.

My feelings on the whole notion were mixed. I've never been the soapbox type, and the idea of living with so much zeal made me slightly uncomfortable. On the other hand, if our kids weren't interested in saving the world, it probably wouldn't get saved.

The prospects of my day were a bit less optimistic. Karl Vogel's memorial service was scheduled for eleven a.m. I understood his body had been released after the autopsy on Sunday and cremation had been his choice.

I put on a chaste navy-blue dress, low heels, and pearl earrings that just showed under my mop of reddish hair. The vivid outdoor colors of summer were appropriately subdued by a gray sky that cooled the day and provided a break from the recent heat spell.

By eleven a few hundred of us punctual souls had gathered at a Presbyterian church in one of the many surprisingly ruralish areas of the Main Line. Up front a bronze urn sat on a table surrounded by a prodigious quantity of white mums and gladiolus. I chose a seat in the back in order to observe the other mourners.

Linda wore black, including a veiled black hat that may have been in style during her mother's day. It allowed the accused ex-wife to mask her more private emotions, such as embarrassment or terror over being ogled by the crowd. A lace handkerchief took care of any sniffles or sobs. I felt genuinely sorry for the woman. Any way you looked at it, she was having one of the toughest days of her life.

Timothy Bedoes did the honors at her elbow. He wore the navy pin-striped suit I originally met him in, and with his shirt cuffs buttoned and jacket on, he looked quite dignified despite those improbable teeth.

Nancy Carlino was in attendance as well as her successor, Akeesha–seated on opposite sides of the room, however.

In a pew about right center, meek Darlene Polk appeared lost without the fortifying presence of her greyhound.

Colin Greene carried his youngest boy, who wore short black pants and a pale-gray jacket. I supposed the other children had been left behind to mind the hardware store. When Greene caught sight of me, he blinked with surprise; understandable since I had misled him with my yarn about a make-believe anorexic daughter.

With Annie Snellenberg there was no such danger. All my information about her had been garnered from her neighbor. Yet, despite her bulk, I almost missed noticing her–the church was that crowded.

Police were in evidence–the one from the autopsy and, if my observations were accurate, a few others as well.

I also recognized Linda's employees–the assistant-trainer Roxanne, and Victor the capable handyman, although he sat so far back I'm sure he couldn't hear a word of the eulogy. Located several rows ahead of him, I couldn't understand much either; and English was my one and only language.

I probably should have spent my time reflecting about Karl Vogel; but he refused to come into focus for me. Perhaps I was still assimilating the negative information I'd been collecting, weighing it with Linda's admission that she still loved the man. But maybe like a lot of people, funerals simply sent my imagination off into space.

I amused myself by trying to guess who had been clients of Karl, who were family, who were friends, potential lovers, police, etc.

Other times I merely gazed out the tilted-open stained-glass windows beside me. A cluster of English sparrows pecked at some food on the ground, maybe a cookie dropped by one of the few children at the service. Sun shimmered off Linda's dark Lincoln, which was parked in the far right row of cars, while at the back edge of the lot a breeze rippled the pines shading Victor's derelict station wagon. With a little mental exercise I remembered that Bedoes drove something low and dark green, and I endured another of the minister's sickly sweet sentences by scanning the lot for its parking space.

Just as I was about to check on my suspects again, the clergyman suggested we all rise and bow our heads. During the murmur and rustle of feet I heard a whooshing noise and thought I noticed a flash of light out in the parking lot.

"Dear Lord," the minister began.

"Fire!" someone shouted.

I glanced out to see flames curling from the trunk of Linda's car.

The congregation panicked. People bolted for the rear of the church. Others pushed past the minister toward the doors on either side of the pulpits. Some who were stuck in the middle of the room began climbing over the pews.

Way too late, a policeman jumped up on a pew and made himself ridiculous by shouting, "Everybody remain calm. Exit in an orderly fashion." He couldn't see the fire from his side of the room, or he would have shouted, "Get away from the windows."

When the boom came, debris and smoke burst into the

building on the gust. A couple of the stained-glass windows cracked. Women screamed. Men gasped and bellowed. In a practiced motion the minister ushered people out the front by their elbows, except this time in fast-forward.

I rubbed my stinging eyes and climbed up onto my seat. Linda's car had been far enough from the building when it exploded to keep injuries from flying particles to a minimum. In fact, nobody needed help that I could see; so I used my vantage point to search the chaos for my suspects.

With his young son slung over his shoulder, Colin Greene stepped across the seats of the pews as if he'd had fireman training. He looked determined to prevent Karl Vogel from posthumously claiming another of his children.

Nancy Carlino? Stuck in traffic but about as surprised and put out as anybody else.

Her face pinched from worry and perhaps painful feet, Darlene Polk brought up the rear of the crowd exiting the center aisle. As she shuffled forward, her body swayed and her hands plucked each other. A brief self-satisfied smile made me wonder whether she was the bomber–but maybe life had simply proven her pessimistic view correct yet again.

Victor. Victor was gone. Before I could even glance his way, he had managed to exit the church, circle the fire, get in his car, and leave.

Annie Snellenberg, however, was the sole person seated exactly as she had been before the commotion. Unprepared or unable to run to safety, she seemed reconciled to dying on the spot or at least waiting out the rush. This was a dimension to obesity I had not yet considered–the simple physical danger brought on by restricted mobility.

It also occurred to me that Annie might have planted the fire bomb and was enjoying a good gloat. She did work for a construction company, and construction work sometimes involved explosives.

When the church was nearly empty, I approached the front of the room where Timothy Bedoes and Linda stood. Linda looked bloodless and dizzy while her attorney seemed cool, albeit inconvenienced. In the near distance a siren wailed.

"What happened?" Linda asked first me, then Timothy. "What happened?"

"Somebody's torched your car," I answered.

"They wanted to kill me?" She was incredulous, shocked.

Tim's glance told me he would field that one. "No, no. Probably not. A warning, that's all. You must know something threatening. From a defense standpoint it might actually be good. Let's find somewhere to talk." He jostled her out of her stupor and guided her away from me, perhaps because one of the men I'd pegged as a cop was approaching.

Gauging that a colleague would get to Linda and Bedoes eventually, the officer settled for me. "I noticed you looking out the window. Did you see anyone near that car?"

"No one."

"What did you see?"

I told him everything, including Annie Snellenberg's possible access to explosives, which he dutifully wrote down; and when I turned around, Linda and Bedoes were out of sight. Elsewhere, others were being questioned, including the minister.

When I finally got outside, the firemen had already completed their task. Linda's sleek blue Lincoln was now a deformed, charred mess of steaming, stinky metal.

Sooty black ashes had also landed on my windshield. The wipers just left smears, so I rubbed a spot clean with a crumpled newspaper from the back seat.

Soon enough, the monotony of driving home would help me organize my impressions.

And soon enough I realized I didn't have enough information to make sense of the "warning." With the exception of Victor's hasty escape, none of the suspects had done anything particularly suspicious after the fire started.

Passing by Bryn Derwyn on the way home, something jogged in my memory. Something prompted by a conversation I had at the Moats's dinner party. The doctor, Pam, had been talking about strong emotions and how passive-aggressives got their way. She expected me to state the obvious.

"Remote control," I had responded. *Remote control.*

Chapter 22

HOPING LINDA would still be asleep, I dropped by her house about eight-thirty Wednesday morning.

Loud music poured into the drive from the detached garage, and that's where I found Victor kneeling on his left knee, resting his elbow on his right, a nice heavy wrench clasped in his sooty hand. Bad timing on my part. He appeared to be changing the spark plug in a mower.

I turned down the radio on the work shelf, raising my eyebrows to ask if I could turn it off completely. The Vogels' shared handyman shrugged his assent.

"Ms. Arden iz not awake," he informed me. His parenthetical moustache drew my attention to his mouth, away from his scarred skin. "Come back later?" Without his hat his remaining straight black hair lay wet across his pate. He wore another set of khaki pants and shirt, but these were grease-stained and already sweaty. Tonight's camp cookout at Bryn Derwyn promised to be unpleasantly hot.

"Victor," I said with both sympathy and concern, "I noticed you left the church very quickly yesterday." The use of his name startled him, also the fact that I'd been observing his actions during the memorial service. "May I ask why?"

His face hardened.

"The police must have noticed, too."

Mentioning the police seemed to cause Victor physical pain, and I remembered Linda telling me how carefully he avoided contact with the authorities.

"Are you an illegal?" I asked, not really expecting a truthful answer.

To my surprise, he replied, "Oh, no. Citizen. Dr. Karl helped me." The man's expressive face warmed when he spoke his former employer's name, so I shifted the conversation accordingly.

"Dr. Vogel was good to you then?"

Victor relaxed onto a nearby low stool and eyed me with reluctance. Clearly, he wished I would go away, but just as clearly he feared I could somehow cause him trouble. He would endure my questions long enough to gauge my intentions.

"Yes, good," he answered. "When I arrived Miami from Cuba," which he pronounced Cooba, "work very hard to find. Everybody think Victor Marielito. One hunnerd thousand refugees okay people. Twenny thousand Marielitos, you understand?"

"Yes." If my memory of past events served, he was telling me he came to America during the Mariel boatlift and that 100,000 ordinary Cubans escaped as well as the 20,000 career criminals who gave them all a bad name. Snide jokes proliferated at the time, often with "Marielitos," in the punch line.

"No work until I come north and meet Dr. Karl."

So, he had every reason to be loyal to the man and no apparent reason to betray him. Unless there were aspects to the story Victor wasn't telling. If, for example, Victor *had* been a career criminal and Karl used the information to his own advantage...

"What about Ms. Arden? Has she been good to you, too?"

Victor shook his head with sadness. "Very sorry about Ms. Arden. Nice lady."

"Good morning, Gin," said a female voice, Linda's. "And thank you, Victor, for the kind words."

The man abruptly stood. Yet he was too embarrassed to reply, if his drooping head and rocking feet told me anything.

Linda watched me, waiting for an explanation.

"Victor said you were still asleep, so we were just shooting the breeze."

Linda eased the irritation out of her forehead with her fingers, jiggling curls as she did so. "Sorry, Gin. This whole business has me paranoid. Come on in. I'll make you a cup of coffee."

Then it occurred to me she must have come out to the garage for a reason. Also, she was dressed for going out–cuffed linen shorts and a silk T-shirt. "Did you need Victor for something?" I asked.

She nodded. "To pick up the rental car with me. But we can go later."

"Why don't I take you?" That way I could be useful and ask my questions, too.

Linda looked at the spark plug mess her employee was involved with and shrugged. "That'd be great, if you don't mind."

A moment or two later we were on our way to rent a replacement for the torched Lincoln. The silence was comparable to driving my kids to their various obligations–baseball games, shoe store, dentist. Quizzing them in that captive situation always reminded me of spearing fish in a tank; but kids can be slippery, and you have to make use of your advantages.

"Did you notice Victor left the church in a hell of a hurry yesterday?" I opened.

Linda blinked. "He did?"

"Yes, he did. Of course, he was sitting right in the back so nobody was in his way."

We stopped at a corner, and I noticed Linda staring at me. "What are you getting at?" she asked.

"Just wondering. Was he as fond of Karl as he said he was?"

Now she got it. Her mouth opened and closed, and her dark eyes widened. "You think Victor had something to do with Karl's death?"

"You tell me."

She thought about that while I turned the corner. "Phew. Victor. I don't know. I guess he could have had something against Karl. Maybe he picked something up while he was working at the old place."

"Blackmail? Karl wouldn't pay?"

"I don't know, Gin. Anything's possible."

"Your ex-husband is dead," I reminded her. "And your car was bombed."

"Phew. Yeah. How can I forget?"

I braked for a light. Business traffic briskly crossed our path right and left.

"What's Victor's last name?" I asked. "He said he came over during the Mariel boatlift. Maybe Bedoes can find out more about him."

"De la Nuez. Victor de la Nuez." She spelled it for me. "But wouldn't the police already be checking into him?"

I shrugged. "Maybe. Maybe now." I meant since the fire bomb. Before they were certain they already had the guilty party.

De la Nuez. A nice name. A nice, interesting name.

So where had I seen it before?

Chapter 23

I MADE CERTAIN Linda got together with her replacement transportation, then I went to the Wonder Bread outlet to buy a hundred and eighty hamburger rolls and just as many hot dog rolls. From there I proceeded to the Wayne Acme where I loaded up with the ingredients for six pans of chocolate chip cookie bars and enough paper plates and cups to fill a shopping cart. As an afterthought, I grabbed a few heads of lettuce, five pounds of tomatoes, and three large white onions.

Today was July 3, the date of Bryn Derwyn Day Camp's annual family cookout. Why they served the traditional Fourth of July food so close to the holiday I couldn't say, unless it was because most kids could be relied on to eat the stuff. A pretty good reason, come to think of it.

Anyway, the parents were expected at three, or as soon as they could break away from work. They would play a few games with the kids, eat the burgers, baked beans, hot dogs, and dessert, play a little more, and everybody would go home about dark.

With Patty Hepple still recovering from appendicitis, the young in-house camp director had her hands more than full buying the rest of the food from the school's regular suppliers; coaxing Jacob, Bryn Derwyn's maintenance guru, to set up a grill; and badgering the counselors to set up the games. All that while eighty campers scurried around scraping knees and picking fights and otherwise flirting with mayhem. Running a couple of errands and baking a few batches of cookie bars struck me as the least I could do to help.

Timothy Bedoes's phone call caught me opening a box of yellow cake mix to start the third batch of cookie bars. (My real cookies always *always* come out burned on the bottom and raw on top.)

"Tough day," the attorney opened.

"I'll say." I emptied the water from the measuring cup of shortening for batch number three and dumped the remaining white lump in the bowl with the mix before I realized Bedoes referred to the fire at the memorial service yesterday.

"But things are looking up. The girlfriend Linda said she was spying on confirmed she and Karl spent Sunday night together at his house, which puts Linda at the crime scene the morning before his death and not the same day."

"If the jury believes that."

"I think they will. It's progress anyway."

"How about the girlfriend? Is she a possibility?"

"Not really. She's terrified of dogs, so the idea of her handling a pit bull just won't wash. Also, their affair was too new to go that sour."

"Too bad," I remarked.

"Getting nervous?"

"We don't really have a number one suspect, except maybe Victor." For a second the clattering of chocolate chips pouring into the bowl interfered with my concentration.

"Who?" Bedoes asked.

"Victor de la Nuez, Karl and Linda's all-purpose employee."

"Ah, the Cuban."

"Former Cuban. Karl helped him to become an American citizen." I explained about the Mariel boatlift connection and the possibility Victor might have tried unsuccessfully to pressure Karl in some way.

"And de la Nuez retaliated? Very interesting theory. Very interesting. The judge certainly steered me right when he put me onto you."

I sighed as much from the overblown flattery as from

the effort of stirring batter moistened only by eggs and a little melted butter. "We can't guess what his grievance might be, but it doesn't mean he couldn't have had one."

"…that he thinks Linda knows about," Bedoes added. "I'll look into his background right away. What else do you have going on?" Besides a cookout for eighty campers and their parents?

"Pit bulls," I answered, plunking batter onto a greased ten-by-thirteen-inch pan. Spreading it around was more effort than I could manage with a phone tucked between my shoulder and my ear, so I ceased production.

"Doc and I discussed trying to connect one of the suspects to a local pit bull breeder, but the idea went nowhere. Those dogs mostly seem to be available from suspicious characters *for* suspicious characters."

"Hummm," said the lawyer evasively.

My mind felt a nudge from its subconscious counterpart, yet no helpful thought came into focus, just something blurry about Victor and dogs…

Meanwhile, Bedoes the Brusque Attorney had gone a bit soft on me and was inquiring about his client's health.

I assured him I had seen her that morning, and she looked fine.

"Good, good," he said with what I assessed to be genuine relief.

Which reminded me that flowers bloom in all sorts of mulch.

The afternoon remained a trifle warm, maybe eighty-six or -seven, but parents valiantly shed their business clothes in the boys' and girls' rooms and emerged to play with their kids in T-shirts, shorts, and sandals. By four there were nearly a hundred and seventy adults and children playing Wiffle-Ball baseball, horseshoes, badminton, and Ping-Pong on the front yard of the sprawling brick school. On the hill to the left of the drive, the smaller kids enthralled Mom and Dad with tricks on the jungle-gym. Others got pushes on the five swings.

While carrying a case of cold sodas out from the refrigerator, I overheard one dimpled girl state, "and this is where we keep our lunches," as if she had maneuvered her mother into a tour of every area in the school she had ever entered. Later I heard the girl boasting about the cement- block rectangle rising from the mud to the right rear of the main building.

"That's where they're putting the new gym, but we're not allowed to play in the dirt."

Her mother nodded as if she, too, was slightly disappointed; and I thought of my grandmother's comment about me raising my mother. Could I possibly have sounded like the dimpled girl?

Anticipating dinner at five, at four-thirty I lit the big charcoal grill Jacob had assembled in the front circle. Rip had accepted the role of chef, an honor his family rarely bestowed upon him. Steak and London broil he had down to a science, but hamburgers he flattened with the spatula until the juice squished out. He also over-melted the cheese until it all but dripped off, and hot dogs—hot dogs he burned into ghosts of their former selves. I intended to hang around and ever-so-tactfully offer him opened buns when the food looked ready.

He had just slapped down twenty burgers when I noticed a sign being brandished by an eight-year-old boy with freckles and skinned knees. "Cows have feelings, too," it read. The boy began to march around Rip, me, and the grill.

Another camper joined him with "Pigs up, Hot dogs down." The girl had cleverly traced her feet, toes up, to decorate the middle of her effort.

"Save the rainforests," read the sign by a taller boy wearing an oversized Virginia Lacrosse T-shirt, "Meat is murder," claimed another sign.

Rip's face glowed as brightly as the charcoal. "Where is she?" he sputtered *"Where is she?"*

In my stunned state, I foolishly asked, "Who?"

"You know who."

My husband handed me his spatula and stalked through the school's front doors in search of the offending temporary counselor. I couldn't decide who to pity more– Rip or Stevie Luckenbill.

More campers carrying more protest signs emerged from the building. One mother folded her arms and bit her lip in consternation. A father took his son aside to ask what was going on. Soon there was a distinct division between Them and Us.

"What will you do?" one mother asked me.

A second woman lamented, "I've got thirty relatives coming for chicken tomorrow. Amy better not pull this then."

Yet another threw up her hands. "Joey, put that sign down and come get your dinner." A small scuffle ensued.

Rip re-emerged from the building with a certain very determined look on his face. He had decided to vent his anger after giving the matter some thought, an extraordinary use of self-control and one that almost always got him exactly what he wanted.

Looking at the hamburgers shriveling on the grill, my own feelings were mixed, but I tended to feel sorry for Stevie Luckenbill.

I later learned she had been unable to stay for the cookout, so our daughter filled in by handing out art supplies. The slogans on the signs had been generated by the campers themselves.

"Listen, folks," Rip shouted, his temper completely under control. "I'm sorry about the disruption, but I think we can take care of everybody here. Gin?" His eyes implored me to tell everyone how we were going to take care of them.

I searched the crowd in vain for the woman who was supposed to be in charge. The in-house director was forty feet away helping a boy climb down from a tree. I took a deep breath and loudly announced, "Grilled cheese and tomato sandwiches for whoever wants them. Hamburgers and hot dogs for everybody else."

In the corner of my eye I noticed a very contrite Chelsea speaking to each camper as she collected their signs. Rip had shifted into the mollify-the-parents routine he did so well. I turned the burgers and withheld the cheese. When Garry approached, I begged him to stuff tomato and the diverted cheese slices into the empty hamburger and hot dog rolls. These I toasted ever-so-slightly over the coals.

Soon a line formed with people grasping flimsy white paper plates. These quickly filled with food. Dinner was served, just not exactly as planned.

When our hundred and seventy people had more or less been fed and idle games had resumed around the fringes of the lounging families, Rip sidled over for a private word with me. Chelsea and Garry sat on the grass to my left and right. Garry nibbled a cookie bar.

"What could be worse?" Rip remarked, spreading his hands to encompass the afternoon's near-fiasco.

"Stevie Luckenbill coming to our Fourth of July picnic?" I asked rhetorically.

Chelsea sat upright so quickly the hairs on my arm prickled.

"She is, Mom. Didn't I tell you?"

Chapter 24

"WHAT...ARE...you...talking...about?" I challenged our daughter. I had been lounging between my kids on the school's front lawn, but I jumped up to stand beside my husband.

Chelsea's chin lifted in such swift defiance that her golden-red curls flew. "You invited her yourself, Mom. I heard you."

"When?"

"That day Stevie drove Garry and me home. You invited her for dinner. Don't you remember? And she couldn't stay, so you said, 'Some other time.' So why can't tomorrow be the other time? What's the big deal?"

"The big deal is you're supposed to ask me before you invite anyone over."

"Now take it easy," Rip soothed. "You both have a point. But Chelsea, your mother's right. She's the hostess and the cook, and she should be consulted before you create more work for her. In the future both you kids should remember that. It's common courtesy. Okay?"

Both our kids nodded grudgingly.

"But what about tomorrow?" Chelsea whined. "Stevie was going to bring her boyfriend and everything. I wanted to introduce them to Aunt Didi and Grammy Struve."

"Un-invite them," Garry suggested.

The rest of us shot him a glare, and he lay back on the school's front grass and closed his eyes.

"Obviously we can't do that," Rip reasoned. "We'll have to let it go this time." He raised an eyebrow at me, tacitly asking me to cope with the family flux once again.

"Yeah, yeah, yeah," I caved in. Then I looked at my watch. "Just enough time to stop at a book store and the

Acme before they close." Even if they were open on the
Fourth, I chose not to be there. "You guys will have to
clean up here."

Rip asked what I needed so urgently at the store.

I tilted my head toward the now-dead grill. "Stevie
Luckenbill's a vegan–remember?" I waited while my
husband puffed and rolled his eyes, then I elaborated. "So
tomorrow, we all are."

The local bookstore was out of Mollie Katzen's
highly recommended *Moosewood Cookbook,* so I picked
up a couple of vegetarian magazines and hoped to heaven
there would be enough recipes in them to get me through
a meatless Fourth of July for eleven.

Sitting with my windows open in the nearest Acme
grocery store parking lot, I scanned the recipes hoping for
something I could a) imagine myself eating and b)
potentially bring off without practice.

The more I read, the more I panicked. Lulled by
unintimidating titles such as "Raspberry Mousse" or
"Eggplant and Tomato Gratin," I soon discovered a
glaring deficiency in my education. Most of the
ingredients had never been mentioned at the Cynthia
Struve School of Cooking–items such as "agar-agar
flakes" and that curiously religious-sounding "balsamic"
vinegar.

Fortunately, the magazine editors realized a few
Cynthia Struve graduates remained among the general
public, because many of the items were followed by a
parenthetical "see glossary." Tempeh, mirin, tamari, and
udon noodles, for example–none of them anything my
mother ever touched with a fork. To my knowledge. Pigs'
feet and scrapple–yes. Glue cheese and corn meal mush–
yes. Asiago, arborio, hijiki, or masa harina–probably not.

And yet I might have forged ahead except for the
second presumption (the first being that I could read the

recipes). Everything seemed to require bags full of those mysterious ingredients and oodles of preparation time.

"This is not going to work," I told the parking lot, which was emptying in anticipation of sundown. Realizing I would have to muddle through with a menu I already knew how to prepare, I left the car and took a cart inside the store. Lettuce, celery. I could cope with those. Maybe I'd buy macaroni salad, too. Did Stevie eat mayonnaise? Rolls. Did she eat butter? Spaghetti? Tomato sauce with no meat?

I grabbed a bag of spinach for spinach lasagna–skip the egg in the cottage cheese, skip the bacon. I put the spinach back.

Basil. Aha! The pesto Genovese recipe with the fresh basil and pine nuts. I had recently bought my first bottle of olive oil for that, a leap of faith if I ever. What on earth does "extra virgin" mean?

My menu decisions made, I scrambled around for half an hour, then closed my eyes to the cost at the checkout counter. I felt better, optimistic even. Tomorrow night would truly be a celebration worthy of fireworks, a "Boom" Fourth of July, as my father used to say.

Provided that my own new invitee, retired forensic pathologist Dr. Mathias Fleming, refrained from talking business at the table.

For a number of reasons, I wear cheap clothes. First of all, I can afford them. Also, if I forget I'm already dressed for company and wipe soap suds on my thighs, probably nothing will get ruined.

Thursday, July Fourth, I was so nervous about my vegetarian picnic fare I splashed extra-virgin olive oil on the front of my favorite white blouse. It wasn't the stain I was worried about, because long ago somebody told me that Victoria's Secret sells an exceptionally good stain remover (perhaps that *was* Victoria's secret), and I knew the blouse would eventually be returned to the fold as good as new.

The problem was I didn't have anything else to bring out the white in the tiny Swiss dots of my favorite navy summer slacks. Consequently, at four p.m. when our guests were due, I was still upstairs making laundry piles with the contents of my dresser drawers.

"Hurry up, Mom," Chelsea trilled up the stairs, the same way I announced that her school bus was due.

"Be right down," I shouted, then muttered to myself, "Where the hell is my green T-shirt?"

"Hi," said a female voice from the doorway.

I jumped and whirled to find Didi lounging against the jamb.

"What are you doing here?" I asked.

"I was invited," my best friend stated calmly. "More to the point–what are you doing?" She eyed my pink panties and white bra with amused disapproval.

The best defense is a good offense, particularly when nearly nude. I narrowed my eyes. "I'm trying to find my green T-shirt."

"Kelly green? Three buttons at the neck?" Didi asked.

"Yes. And when did you find time to memorize my wardrobe?"

"Don't flatter yourself. Chelsea's wearing a shirt just like that."

"Oh." I sank onto our unmade bed and tried not to whimper. All I wanted was for things to go right once in a while. For balance. For incentive. You bake cookies and they come out just right. Your kids grab a handful and kiss you on the cheek just like in a fifties sitcom.

Or your kelly-green T-shirt is folded right there in the drawer when you need it, and the right person gets arrested for murder. A world in which your daughter asks permission before inviting strangers to dinner or borrowing your clothes.

Fat chance.

Didi had begun to rummage through my discards as if she was going to dress me. Great. I folded my hands and crossed my ankles and admired her graceful movements as she flicked through my belongings.

Her silky blond hair was up in a flawless French twist, ballerina-style, lending her a borrowed classiness not unlike my inexpensive ensembles. Didi the eternal chameleon. I suspected that all her poses were borrowed except the one she struck with me.

Or perhaps they were all real. Pity the psyche of the dog who had to cope with all those Didis. Chivas Beagle, the only known canine psychopath...

Not funny. What a wreck I was today!

"Put these on," Didi ordered in a passable imitation of my mother.

Fortunately, the chosen items were nothing Cynthia would have picked, a shirt in peach linen I usually kept far, far away from the kitchen and fresh white jeans worn only thrice a season simply because they required ironing. Didi also handed me a silver belt and silver Kmart sandals I once bought to disguise myself as Cleopatra.

"Why not shorts?" I asked.

Didi's outfit consisted of new designer jeans and a long-sleeved white silk blouse. The value of the gold jewelry peeking from under tendrils of blond and rattling at the throat of her blouse could have supported an evening at Bookbinder's pricey seafood restaurant for the entire starting team of the Philadelphia Eagles–an evening Didi would thoroughly enjoy, come to think of it.

"The Fourth of July always gets cold," she pointed out.

"True." I recalled many a Fourth shivering on a lawn

chair while trying to balance a paper plate. No matter what the rest of the summer did, the Fourth in Philadelphia couldn't be trusted.

"Mom!" Chelsea hollered up the stairs, sounding even more like me in the mornings.

"Be right down, dear," I said, setting a good example.

"So why the stage nerves?" Didi asked. We were hip to hip putting lipstick on at my bathroom mirror.

"Linda Arden's coming. My mother. A forensic pathologist I just met, and his son, who is a pediatric podiatrist. Hands off, by the way."

"Why?"

"They're mine, okay?"

Didi shrugged. She would do whatever she pleased. As usual.

"So why the stage nerves?" She knew me too well.

"Truth?"

"What else is there?"

Your whole life? But that wasn't fair, or necessarily accurate. "Stevie Luckenbill," I said.

Didi's eyebrow arched. "You never get nervous when you entertain. I've seen you sling hash for seventy-five and remain as cool as Martha Stewart. Stevie who? He must be a hunk. Oh, I can't wait."

I sighed. "Stevie is not a hunk. Stevie is female. A little blond fireball of a woman I accidentally met in connection with Karl's murder who is presently working at Bryn Derwyn's day camp. The kids love her."

"But you don't."

I screwed up my face. "I don't dislike her. She just makes me uncomfortable."

"Why?"

"So much energy. So many convictions. She's exhausting. Also, she's vegetarian, and I've never cooked for..."

"She's not coming," Didi interrupted.

"What?"

"Not coming. I overheard Rip on the phone downstairs. When he got off, he said, 'Oh, good. Maybe now we can have hamburgers.'"

We gathered like a regular bunch of adults on the patio off the living room. Mother lounged decorously on the chaise. Her white hair was bigger than usual, and for once her glasses were devoid of dust. Beneath her pink, two-piece polyester knit pants outfit peeked red sandals housing toenails neatly painted pink. She represented the prototypical Ludwig woman out on the town, endearingly flawed and totally oblivious. I adored her even as I squirmed.

Unaware of either my love or my discomfort, she sipped lipstick prints onto her wine glass while batting her sparse eyelashes up at Dr. Mathias Fleming. I figured the man had a PhD--he could fend for himself.

I wasn't so sure about his son Toby.

"So you take care of children's feet?" Didi asked him. Doc and his son wore matching docksiders without socks. The elder Fleming had gone the wrinkled madras slacks/pink golf shirt route while Dr. Fleming the younger–Toby–displayed nicely suntanned knees beneath baggy khaki shorts covered with enough pockets and snapped pouches to go on safari.

"Yes," he answered. Beneath wavy tan hair, his round, ingenuous, all-American face exhibited no discernible guile or humor, just an ordinary cute nose.

"What do you do if they're ticklish?" Didi inquired.

Dr. Toby Fleming had been breathing, rocking on his docksiders and just breathing with his drink in one hand and the other hand in one of his many pockets. At Didi's remark all these activities halted. When they resumed a moment later, Toby Fleming was back in high school.

"I… I…"

Didi regarded him through half-closed eyes. "Never mind," she said. "I can imagine."

Toby Fleming choked on his own saliva, wiped his mouth, and turned to talk to Garry, who was folded on the ground tying his sneaker. To all appearances they struck up a conversation about how to tie a bow, but whatever they were saying, it engrossed Toby Fleming entirely.

Linda arrived late enough that Rip was busy lighting the bug-repellant torches. I had already displayed my vegetarian culinary efforts on the picnic table. Tossed salad, pesto Genovese with ziti, sliced tomatoes with mozzarella, French bread and butter, and corn on the cob.

"Sorry," Linda told me privately. Her hushed embarrassment competed with a schoolgirl blush. "I almost didn't make it." Her eyes implored me to understand.

"No need to apologize," I assured her.

"It's just…"

"'I know," I said, putting a hand on her arm. "I'm glad you decided to join us. We're a screwy bunch, but we're all on your side."

She sighed all over. "Thanks. You really are a good friend." Our gazes met and sealed the deal.

A few feet away my mother laughed, reminding me to forgive her flaws. We really were all in this together, just as she had shown me, just as I'd been learning for myself.

Back in the fenced part of the yard, Gretsky and Chevy frolicked like a pair of idiots. Awkwardness momentarily at bay, Chelsea stood listening to Mother and Doc. Our daughter looked so elegant and lovely that my throat clenched. Over by the lilac bush Toby Fleming watched Garry demonstrate his skill with a hackysack as if he wanted to learn how.

I scooped a mound of salad onto a paper plate and

handed it to Linda. Mosquitoes buzzed by my ear. "Our vegetarian guest canceled at the last minute," I explained. "We're stuck with her rabbit food."

Linda's face transformed into something beautiful. "Load it on, then," she told me. "My nervous system needs all the fuel it can get."

"Where is this Stevie girl you promised?" my mother came over to ask. She picked up a plate and began to help herself. "She sounds so interesting."

"Her boyfriend's sick," I said. Rip had related the message earlier. "Summer cold or something. Anyway, he feels too rotten to be with people."

Mother clucked. "Too bad. You've done such a nice job with the food." That was when I decided it actually was a "Boom" Fourth of July, Barnes-style. Going en masse to Radnor High to watch the fireworks in the school van Rip borrowed was icing on the cake.

ASLEEP, MOST likely smiling over a contented dream, the phone awoke me at two A.M.

"Ms. Barnes?" said a squeaky young voice.

"Yes?"

"It's Stevie. Can you please tell Mr. Barnes I can't come to work tomorrow?"

I sat up straight on the edge of the bed. Behind me Rip twisted to listen.

"Sure, Stevie. But what's wrong?" Her voice sounded worried, perhaps even scared.

I waited through some gulps and ragged gasps that finally ended in a sob. "I'm...I'm in jail," she confessed.

And then the sobbing took over completely

Chapter 25

"WHAT HAPPENED?" I all but shouted into the phone. "Are you all right?"

Stevie Luckenbill's sobs struggled to a halt, "I'm okay," she sniffed. "I guess it's my own fault. I mean, I knew it could happen, b u t..."

"What did you do?" I asked.

"Just a sit-in. I probably shouldn't talk about it, you know? The lawyers always say that."

"You have a lawyer?"

"Oh, yeah. From my group. He was there, like in his car, you know? Protecting our rights. That's how come I can use the phone to call you." Because her animal rights organization's lawyer planned ahead.

We sighed in unison.

"What happens now?" I inquired.

"They've got this six-hour arraignment rule, so I'll be seeing a judge pretty soon. Eight A.M. I think is the earliest, so I'll just, you know, be here until then." She sounded as if she thought she expected to be there after the arraignment, too.

"You have any money?" I asked.

"Just what I've saved for tuition."

"Will your boyfriend be able to bring it to you if you need it for bail?"

"Michael doesn't drive."

I made a face in the dark to vent my disbelief. What were the odds of a self-respecting American youth over the age of sixteen not knowing how to drive?

"He can get the money," Stevie amended. "He just can't bring it over."

"Okay," I told her. "Here's what we'll do. You wait there for the arraignment," as if she had a choice, "you find out what bail will cost, and you call me again." I paused to be sure she was listening and not off on some sorry side trip. Behind me, Rip leaned on one elbow, taut and alert.

"Then I'll either pick up the money from Michael or get it from him when I take you home."

Stevie's voice wavered and squeaked, but a modicum of spunk had returned.

"Thank you, Ms. Barnes. I...thank you," she said.

I told her she was welcome.

She called back at eight-thirty to say bail was set at $10,000, which meant she needed $1,000 cash. After she assured me about twenty times she had the money, for my convenience we decided I would withdraw the cash from my bank when it opened at nine. Later I would accompany her to her bank so she could repay me. After all, "Michael *was* sick last night." The summer cold. I could scarcely wait to meet Michael, who–no doubt unfairly–I expected to be a total wimp.

The District Court building was the requisite municipal brick with weeds poking out of the azaleas and ground pine to either side of the front steps. Yews with several untrimmed inches of growth threatened to cut off the light of the front windows, which were shaded by plastic slats anyway. I parked, avoiding the spots reserved for "Police Cars Only," and entered the lobby.

At the edges of an area roughly the size of my kitchen and living room combined, a few people waited nervously on the sturdy captains' chairs. Behind the gray Formica counter spanning the room were five clerical desks occupied by women. A small vase of artificial pink and blue flowers softened the "Please Check in Before Being Seated" and "No Smoking" signs. A dish of candy corn probably several months old waited by the phone either to be consumed or dusted. Walking across the gray tweed carpet, I tried to pretend I was approaching the Sears and Roebuck catalog desk or the counter where you talk to somebody about ordering a sliced ham, but no go.

The mumbles of some orderly courtroom procedure came from an opened room to the left. An invisible male interrupted in tones calculated for his own pleasure. I noticed perhaps twenty-five chairs faced the robed judge up on a platform protected by attractive panels of wood. He appeared to have a gavel on a chain, a phone, a Bible, a TV/ VCR combo, state and federal flags against the wall–the whole bit. I felt intimidated on Stevie's behalf, with some sympathy withheld for after I learned more about what she had done.

"Hello," I told the clerk who met me at the desk. "My name is Ginger Barnes. I'm here to post bail for Stevie Luckenbill."

"Okay," said the woman. She wore gold-rimmed glasses. Her face was lumpy and white, and her dyed dark hair was thinning. However, she smelled like lilies of the valley and her smile was neutrally patient.

"May I ask your name?" Only way to learn it some-times.

She blinked up at me.

"Jean," she said with obvious distrust.

"Listen, Jean," I said. "I'm just Stevie Luckenbill's boss's wife..." I paused long enough for the woman to appreciate how remote my connection to the defendant sounded. "...and I don't really know why she's here. Would you mind filling me in?"

Jean glanced left and right. She set the pen she was holding down on the clipboard she had brought out at the mention of Stevie's name.

"Didn't you hear about the candlelight vigil over at Hill's Pharmaceutical?"

"The local news hasn't been on yet."

Jean gave a little shrug. "Protesting the treatment of the animals. Demanding their release, something to do with the Fourth of July." Independence Day.

The clerk's thin lips pressed together in disapproval as she sniffed in some lily of the valley. "Ms. Luckenbill became quite...difficult when the police tried to disperse the crowd. She actually hit an officer with her fists, kicked him. Tried to scratch him, too."

"Not good."

Jean became indignant. "It's a felony," she said.

"So, the charges are what?"

Jean read from the clipboard. "Disorderly conduct, trespassing, resisting arrest, aggravated assault."

I imagined the judge's looming figure intoning those words from his artificial desk height, a diminutive Stevie Luckenbill down below.

"Anybody else, uh, misbehave in that fashion?" I asked. Jean compressed her lips and wagged her head. "A few resisting arrests, but she was the only felony."

I made a disgusted-mother face, the one that says, "Kids. What can you do?"

Jean's curiosity about human behavior had ceased long ago. She just recounted my twenties and wrote a receipt as if life were a cog railway and we had just moved one notch closer to the ultimate cliff.

"Where is she?" I asked when our business seemed to be concluded.

Jean crooked a thumb toward an officer guarding a door across from the courtroom. He unlocked it at her signal. When Stevie did not emerge, I walked over to look in. Seated on one of three yellow plastic chairs, the young felon rested her head on a fake walnut table. I noticed a pillow on top of a built-in drawer and storage cabinet combo in the opposite corner, but I wouldn't have used it either. Too public, too desperate, too dirty.

"Come on, kid," I told her. "Time to go home."

She lifted her body upright as if all her limbs were stiff. She wore grass-stained jeans and an oversized white sweatshirt that had protested itself out of the last few attempts to throw it in the washer. Her hair flaps, normally so perfectly swept up at the ears, stuck out as if on wires. The rest seemed plastered to her narrow head, making it appear misshapen. Pouches the size of marshmallows protruded above her narrow flat cheeks. The pointy nose shone. Her normally sparkling eyes had gone flat. She looked thirty-five and wasted. I hooked my hand around her elbow and guided her out of the building.

"Get any sleep?" I asked.

A slow wave of the head.

"Was there anywhere to sleep?"

Another slow wave of the head. "Just a bench or the floor. The cell I was in wasn't supposed to be for overnight, but it was so late they said it was a waste of time to take me over to the prison."

Linda had been held overnight at the prison. All things considered, Stevie probably had been better off in a nice, clean private holding cell in our nice, clean local police station. Sleep she could get later.

"You owe me a thousand bucks," I remarked to stave off any impending self-pity. "And an explanation."

"Oh, Ms. Barnes. I'm so sorry." She insisted I drive directly to her bank, which I had had every intention of doing anyway.

That understanding achieved, we stood in woeful silence a moment beside my car. The damp Pennsylvania morning pressed around us, and Stevie hugged herself inside her grubby sweatshirt. I could see she wanted to cry, so I interceded with a couple of chirpy remarks about picking a heck of a night to sit on a hill holding a candle. "How did you keep them lit, anyway?" I asked as I opened the passenger's door.

Stevie actually worked up some enthusiasm and a feeble smile. "We mostly used lighters and flashlights," she answered as she climbed in. "No wax on our fingers and harder to blow out" Since she wasn't heavy enough to flop like a sack of potatoes, she landed inside the Subaru more or less like a bag of grapes.

I rounded to my side and got in.

"Didn't the light attract mosquitoes?" I asked. While we watched the fireworks at Radnor High School, I'd been bit by my share. Garry, our resident sweet-meat, had collected at least a dozen bites in forty-five minutes.

"We were covered up, and I guess there were more of us than them."

I glanced over to meet her weak smile, and I realized she deserved a more equal woman-to-woman attitude from me than the mother-to-daughter approach I'd been using. It wasn't her fault that she would be carded in bars until her hair went white. Some people just don't match their packaging, their voices, their open-eyed s t a r e …

Okay, so Stevie Luckenbill was a bit of an ingénue. She was a legal adult nevertheless, and she had just taken a deliberate risk to promote her beliefs.

"You want to doze off?"

"Thanks," she mumbled. "Wake me up at the bank."

I did. And then I did again at her home.

Situated on a crumbling road outside of Norristown, Stevie's apartment building was an aged stucco block with a rusting plain iron handrail and cement steps that threatened to tilt over onto the sidewalk. It hid from the surrounding tiny private yards behind two mammoth Jerusalem pines, patriarchs of the plant world, balding, doddering, complete with bad breath. Their smell was preferable to the lobby.

Stevie flipped up the unlocked aluminum flap of her

mail cubicle and searched inside with a finger, just an habitual domestic ritual, soothing because of its normalcy. Nothing was there from the holiday. Nothing from today.

When she opened the left front apartment door, an overly painted two-paneled job reading "A" in fake brass, she received a lukewarm greeting from a forty-pound mutt with dull black fur and a standoffish attitude. Her owner had abandoned her overnight.

"Grade," the young woman effused to the dog. "You ole doll baby." Stevie used both hands to jiggle the animal's ruff the way obnoxious aunts wiggle children's cheeks.

Grade's eyes softened. She wagged her tail and eased in for an all-consuming hug.

A line from a Turgenev short story Rip sometimes quoted came to mind: "Animals are infinitely forgiving." The gist of it was that a man foolishly drove himself and his horse too far into a blizzard, most likely a fatal mistake, and the horse forgave him.

It occurred to me that if the implied superiority had merit, no one should tolerate experimentation on unresisting animals, or eat their flesh, or wear their hides. For a second there it hurt to breathe.

Then I heard Stevie's boyfriend sniffle, "Oh, lucky-ducky, I was so worried about you." Yuk. The endearment was no doubt a playful twist on her last name, but yuk.

"It's okay, Michael. I'm fine."

Anyone could see she wasn't fine. She seemed distant and hurt, but Michael wasn't disposed to notice. "How are you?" she asked, and the idiot chose to answer.

"A fever, sniffling, aching. The whole works. You know I would have been there with you otherwise."

Yeah, sure, I thought.

Michael's forehead puckered. His wire-rimmed glasses rose on his nose. He was thin, tall, clad in a long-sleeved plaid shirt and narrow, slept-in bluejeans, socks, no shoes. His nose was as pointy as Stevie's and pink, not fire-engine red, but damp. I made a mental note not to touch any of the furnishings.

There were few furnishings to avoid, I realized. A clothes rack to the right, a mattress with rumpled sheets in a faded blue pattern on the floor directly across from the front door, a bulky old TV on a cheap chrome-and-chipboard stand, a riot of pots and dishes in a kitchen alcove to the left. I supposed the door behind the clothes rack belonged to a bathroom. Grade had her own poodle placemat with a water bowl on it and a hairy plaid dog bed over by the tiny kitchen table, but that was it. I–T, it.

Except for the half-a-dozen used pink tissues overflowing a plastic wastebasket. I really disliked Michael Taylor, for that was his whole name, given to me when Stevie escaped his embrace long enough to introduce us. Easily twelve inches taller than she, his lanky arm draped across her shoulders possessively. Brown hair sprang away from an off-center part. He grinned comfortably now, probably because his caregiver was within reach.

Stevie herself had relaxed into exhaustion. I wanted to swat Michael's arm off her frail shoulder, yell at him to be more considerate, but I forced a smile.

"You don't drive," I remarked.

"No. No, I don't."

I waited, feeling I deserved an explanation. Because of this peculiarity I had, after all, bailed out his girlfriend.

He finally caught wind of my expectation. "Tires," he said. "They contain animal matter."

Rubber tires? The tires they use on cars? My incredulity spawned questions so fast I couldn't put them into words. Did that mean he also scorned bicycles, buses? Did that mean he walked everywhere?

"Don't you even ride in Stevie's Volkswagen?" I managed to ask.

"Umm. Yes, I do," he admitted.

An uncomfortable silence accompanied my mental list of unflattering nouns. "Hypocrite" headed the list, which degenerated into several less-ladylike epithets.

Stevie drew in a breath. "Listen, Mrs. Barnes. Thanks a lot. I'm really grateful…"

"But you need to get some sleep."

She nodded, grateful once again.

Something tugged at my memory. An assignment Rip had given me. Bad news to be delivered.

"Stevie," I said as she began to turn away, her eyes resting longingly on the rumpled bed. She paused, and the woman I had connected with in the car waited stoically for my message.

"I'm sorry, but you can't come back to camp." Rip had been quite specific about that. Raising children's sensibilities was one thing, advocating illegal protests was another. As ludicrous as it seemed to me, she had been charged with a felony. If Rip overlooked that, the parents would lynch him–and rightfully so.

"Nothing personal," I said. "I hope you understand."

"Sure, Ms. B. I get it." She turned again toward the bed, Michael's anchor of an arm turning with her.

The lump in my own throat would ease as soon as I was out the door, but Stevie's dam would probably burst. I was almost–almost–glad she had Michael there.

The morning was full now, heating up with its summer smells. As usual, the cool of the Fourth had been sheer bravado. Afterward our summer always surrendered to the sun's very first threat. Asphalt streets would be bubbling by noon.

Stevie's cash lay heavily in my purse. Her home, her boyfriend weighed heavily in my mind. She had so little to lose and cared so much. Cared fanatically, perhaps. Cared at least enough to kick a police officer, thereby technically committing a felony. She must have been forewarned by her cautious attorney, the one who waited in his car. He would have advised them all, but Stevie alone had chosen not to listen.

I stood on her sidewalk and breathed in some precious free air. Karl Vogel had represented twin horrors to Stevie Luckenbill—a dog trainer who used force, a dietician who advocated the consumption of meat. With provocation like that, I had to wonder.

Just how far might a brash young zealot go?

Chapter 26

I WAS OUT, so I took the opportunity to finish off the morning with errands–redeposit Stevie Luckenbill's thousand dollars, pick up dry cleaning, buy a replacement part for a lamp, fill the propane canister that had been rattling around in my car for a week. Very dull stuff, and as usual I performed the chores on autopilot and allowed my mind to drift off.

Surprisingly, my concerns about Stevie's fanaticism faded and Victor de la Nuez stepped forward for more intense scrutiny. The way he avoided authority made me believe something was off, either in his present or his past. Furthermore, he had been integral to Karl and Linda's environment before Karl's death and remained so even now.

Also, his name still had a familiarity I couldn't quite place. I felt certain it hadn't been mentioned aloud by anyone–when Linda told me his surname, nothing had clicked. And y e t . . .

By the time I headed home for lunch I'd convinced myself I must have seen it or a similar name written somewhere. Probably not in a book, because my current fictional escape was a Dana Stabenow tale set in Alaska with nary a Spanish surname in sight.

Newspaper? More likely, but a shuffling through the discards on the kitchen counter only reminded me of some local politics I chose to ignore, Stevie's sit-in, and the latest antics of an extroverted entertainer.

Still, a news clipping was the most likely place I would have seen the name.

Halfway through a Lebanon-bologna and pretzel-stick sandwich it came to me. Chelsea's animal-rights scrapbook! I gulped down a cold glass of milk and set off to find my daughter's project, which I located under a Justin Bieber CD on her bedroom desk.

Chelsea's enthusiasm for the project had been brief–only the items she selected on that first weekend were taped to the pages of a red ring binder. Standing at the desk, I reread through them with care–the Sigourney Weaver interview about the ants, the political fuss about the location of some hog farms in North Carolina, the sentencing of the local men who set a pit bull on a defenseless dalmatian.

An item on the fourth page set my limbs to tingling. I pulled out Chelsea's chair and sat down to read the article a second time. Soon I was grinning and blushing and joyously pounding my fists on the desk. Then I stood up and stamped my feet and clutched the notebook to my chest.

Scarcely two months before, a Luis de la Nuez had been arrested along with two other men for staging dog fights in the basement of a house in North Philadelphia.

The name was partly wrong, of course. Karl and Linda's employee's first name was Victor, but no matter. The coincidence of someone named de la Nuez being involved in dog fighting and Karl's fatal attack by a dog was far too astonishing to dismiss. This had to be the pivotal connection I needed. Getting proof would be quite a feat, but if I could do that, the rest of the answers surely would fall into place.

The proof part required some intense thought, so I forced myself back into Chelsea's chair and bounced a pencil eraser off the scrapbook for enough minutes to feel like an hour.

All I really wanted was the evidence to clear Linda, and as Dr. Fleming had explained, which meant finding the dog that actually caused Karl's death. I concentrated on that, beginning by inventorying exactly what I knew about dogs.

Not much. My own pampered hedonist was busy snoozing in a sun spot on the living room carpet. Tibor probably remained caged in the midst of other unhappy bite cases waiting out their individual fates. It probably helped that the German shepherd had been accustomed to spending at least some of his time in a kennel.

What about the pit bull, if that was the proper breed, who had been trained to kill Karl? Where was he? And what would be his fate?

Like gamecocks or thoroughbred horses, a dog as well-trained as that would probably be valued by its owner–especially if it was capable of winning money in the ring. So the odds were good the dog with the missing claw and broken tooth still existed somewhere.

Which meant it needed regular attention.

Which in turn meant if the owner could be located, eventually he would have to go to the dog.

The easiest thing to do would be tell the police about the de la Nuez connection and let them get a search warrant for wherever Luis kept his dogs.

And that's exactly what I might have done if I hadn't been missing one vital piece of information: I had no way of knowing for certain whether Luis was any relation whatsoever to Victor.

I tapped and stared a while longer thinking how I could safely determine whether a relationship between Victor and Luis existed. I did have an idea, but it required a helper and a bit of finesse. Still, being indebted to one of Rip's employees seemed preferable to making a fool of myself with the police.

Chelsea's alarm clock informed me it was now one thirty-five. I dug out my cell phone to call Bryn Derwyn.

A substitute secretary whose voice I didn't recognize answered the school's phone and told me Harvey

Serrentino's summer Spanish class was over.

Would Harvey have gone home for lunch? No. I distinctly remembered him parroting Stevie Luckenbill's meat lecture across the school's picnic table. "Doesn't he stay to tutor in the early afternoon?" I asked.

"I don't know," hedged the substitute.

Find out, I wanted to shout into her ear. Instead I said, "Will you please go see? It's urgent that I speak with Mr. Serrentino. Really urgent."

"Okay." If my annoyance fazed her, she did a nice job of pretending it hadn't. Soon an irritated Harvey came on the line. "Yes?" he asked. "What is this?"

"Aren't you supposed to ask who first?"

"Okay. Who is this, and what do you want?"

"It's Gin Barnes, and I need a huge favor."

Harvey heaved a great sigh. "Sorry, Gin. Sue pulled me out of a tutoring session that wasn't going too well."

"You're welcome."

"Heh," he said. Then he waited for my lead. After all, this was a call from his employer's wife; there were pitfalls to consider.

I thanked him for coming to the phone, then I resurrected the old lie that I needed him to help save a dog's life. Telling him over the phone I was trying to exonerate a woman accused of murder might have strained our acquaintanceship.

"Oh?" His interest seemed genuine. He laughed. "Why me?"

I explained that I needed a translator because the man who had critical information regarding the dog was Cuban and preferred to speak Spanish. "Formerly Cuban," I corrected myself. "You're the only person I could think of to help. Please?" I begged. "This is really quite important."

"You're in a hurry, too, from the sounds of it. Is there

more to this than you're telling?"

Perceptive. I began to feel optimistic about my choice of accomplice. "You're right. And I promise to explain."

"Pick me up at two. And please don't be late." Apparently, summer school was tough on everybody.

I FOUND the forty-year-old teacher lounging on the school's front bench when I arrived–promptly, as requested.

I hopped out of the car to greet him, once again concluding that his lumpy, irregular features and fine light-brown hair were homely enough to be cute. Today he happened to have on baggy tan walking shorts, and I noticed a boyish scar on his left knee that never showed when he wore slacks.

Resting on his elbows, he regarded me with blinking hazel eyes. Was he too nervous to stand? Or was he worried about how our meeting might look from Rip's office windows twenty yards away?

I decided to be honest; it was quicker than tact.

"It isn't a dog we're saving," I said. "It's his owner. She's a friend of mine."

Harvey's eyes blinked faster, and the hands he clasped loosely between his legs twitched.

"Does that matter?" I asked.

The Spanish teacher stood and hooked his thumbs on his shorts pockets. "I should think it matters quite a bit more," he replied, the trace of a wry smile on his lips.

"I didn't want to scare you away."

"Be glad to help if I can." Shyly, he glanced toward Rip's windows, then scraped a pebble off the bottom of one of his black rubber flip-flops. I noticed his toes looked very clean and white, and I suddenly worried he wouldn't be able to sell himself as sleazy, a job requirement I would soon find myself explaining in great detail.

A handful of giggling campers guided by my daughter Chelsea came toward us across the school's front circle. Glancing at them made me notice the front lawn of the school was dotted with small colorful tents of many varieties. I had forgotten about tonight's sleepover—delight of the summer to the kids, dreaded duty for the counselors. My only related chore had been to dig through the garage to find our electric-green bubble tent.

"Chelsea," I shouted. "I'm giving Mr. Serrentino a ride to the train station." Beside me Harvey took a large, much more relaxed breath. "Tell Dad I'll see him later."

"No you won't," Chelsea called back.

"Excuse me," I told Harvey while raising my hand. Then I approached my daughter. "What do you mean I won't see Dad later?"

Chelsea's eyes scrunched into half-moons as she gloated over her answer. "He'll be here," she said smugly, "filling in for Stevie." Apparently, her adolescent mind blamed both her father and me for depriving Stevie's fans of her presence. *That* I would delve into at a later opportunity.

"Good," I concluded. "Then your father won't mind if I borrow his car. Mention it to him when you go inside, will you?"

"Sure," Chelsea agreed with the disdain of the young and intelligent for us daft, older folks.

I parked the Subaru, then proceeded to back Rip's white Mercury sedan out of his reserved spot near the front door.

Harvey climbed in beside me, glancing around at the plush red interior, the papers on the floor, the baseball hat in the back.

"You do still ride the train," I remarked.

"Yes, and thank you," he replied, referring to my fib for appearance's sake. Then he fixed me with an intense expression as if to say, *"If you're not confiding in your husband, this must really be something."*

I drove some distance away from the school before I began to sketch in the details of Linda's situation.

"...so Dr. Fleming and I have determined that someone trained a pit bull to kill Linda's ex-husband, or hired someone to do it. I've got a possible lead on the owner of the dog; but before I go to the police, I need to find out whether a guy named de la Nuez who is known to fight pit bulls is in any way related to the Victor de la Nuez who worked for Karl."

Again, I worried whether Harvey was capable of bringing off his part.

"Have you ever acted?" I asked.

"Don Quixote," he replied proudly. *"Macbeth* back in high school."

Grease or *Streetcar Named Desire* would have been better. Still, it was encouraging that he had pretended to be someone other than himself at least once or twice.

"Well, here's your chance to behave like a thug. You've got to convince Victor de la Nuez your girlfriend is into blood sports." No reply, so I continued, monitoring Harvey's reaction as I went along. "She *loves* football, *adores* boxing, and you thought you'd really get lucky if you took her to a dog fight."

"Are you the girlfriend?" Harvey asked.

"Oh, no," I said. "I'm going to be hiding in the back seat. Victor's seen me and my car a few times too often lately. No, somebody just mentioned Victor's name to you and you made the connection with Luis. You've been wanting to find a dog fight around Philadelphia ever since..."

"...ever since I saw one in Mexico."

"Yes, good. Perfect."

I rolled to a stop at a corner and glanced over at Harvey. He was girding his loins, so to speak. His spine had stiffened, his hands paused in their nervous rubbing, his breath stopped and started whenever he remembered to work his lungs.

"You think you can manage it?" Just watching him I was developing some anxious symptoms myself. How could I have ever been optimistic about this guy?

"Tell me the rest," he instructed.

I couldn't guess whether he was curious for purposes of character motivation or just plain needed distraction from his stage nerves. Still, I told him about everything and everybody, including all I knew about Annie Snellenberg, Darlene Polk, Colin Greene, Nancy Carlino, and Stevie Luckenbill. I sketched in the part about Judge Arden and Timothy Bedoes and ended at the beginning with the story about Linda and Karl's joint ownership of Tibor. I spoke fast and Harvey did not interrupt.

Twenty quick minutes later we entered Chestnut Hill, and I pulled over to let Harvey drive. Then I gave directions from the back until we got to Karl's long driveway, at which time I scrunched myself down into the floor well. I also lifted the one wide armrest between the driver and passenger front seats. That turned the seatback into more of a bench with a shallow, ten-inch-wide depression in the middle.

"Don't drive all the way up to the garage," I warned Harvey, although he had already begun to brake.

"Yes, Mom," he teased. He stopped several yards before the narrow drive widened for parking and turning around.

"There he is," I said. Alas, Victor himself was walking across the drive toward a detached garage tucked behind a tall bunch of yews. The dilapidated station wagon he had driven to the funeral was the only other car in sight, so Akeesha was either off today or she had closed out her job permanently.

"So I noticed. Get down for heaven's sake."

I eyed Harvey from my hiding spot. He appeared exactly the same as his former ineffectual self, only more so. If ever there was a teaching milquetoast, he was it. But before I could suggest we skip the whole thing and go home, Harvey had the car door open and was approaching his prey.

"Hello," the Spanish teacher called. "Hello, there."

I had hoped to go over the plan one last time, maybe say, "Break a leg," the actor's superstitious form of "Good luck." I expected to squeeze Harvey's hand encouragingly and receive some welcome reassurance in return.

Instead I heard flip-flops scrunching on loose gravel and another greeting, this time in Spanish. Victor's fluent response might as well have been babble. Actually, the whole rest of their conversation became a rapid-fire exchange of unintelligible words.

Soon frustrated, I risked a peek through the little gap in the front seat. Several yards ahead of the car the men faced each other in profile to me. As I watched, Harvey wrapped his arm around the former Cuban and possible Marielito, and confided man-to-man, or more accurately geek-to-man-of-the-world.

I understood none of the words, but Victor's don't-touch-me shrug-off and his narrow-eyed dismissal of my emissary set my nerves on edge. Had I unleashed a totally innocent private-school Spanish teacher on a hardened criminal?

I bit my lip. I fidgeted and huffed. I stared and glared and twitched.

Presently the two men stood near Karl's white-on-black hanging office sign, several yards from the stone bench where Akeesha and I had settled down to talk in the sun. Karl's bush-shrouded, immense stone house rose up behind Victor, whose expressions, although shaded by his wide-brimmed hat, came across to me clearly. Resistance predominated.

Harvey faced the former Cuban, back toward me, hands resting patiently on his hips. He used lots of shoulder motion–imploring, deferential movements as if he was half begging, half appealing to his subject's sense of masculine solidarity.

Victor's closed fists pressed against his thighs. His chin rose high. When he spoke, his head snapped back and forth negatively in tempo with his words. I didn't need to hear him to realize he was saying no.

When he actually shouted the word, I nearly jumped out of the car to intervene. Harvey was obviously drowning out there, making a fool of himself and an enemy of Victor. And despite my long-winded lecture, Harvey wouldn't realize–couldn't realize–the danger. My fault. My responsibility.

And yet I simply couldn't risk revealing myself and ruining whatever credibility Harvey might have established. I tried to remember he was an adult. Surely, he could make it back to the car by himself. So what if I was enduring a case of cold sweats?

Finally, Victor held up both hands, palms out. He glared into Harvey's eyes and enunciated slowly this time, word by word. Clearly. Loudly. Emphatically. Although he spoke his original language, no one of any background could mistake his meaning. I was at least twenty yards away, and I quivered.

Please, Harvey. Please get out of there.

Maybe it was genetic memory. Or maybe it was that I'm a woman and probably more physically vulnerable than any but the frailest of men. Possibly it was because I once angered a powerful man who took a swift and very harsh revenge. But seeing Victor's face, hearing his intent, I quaked with exactly the same fear as during my brief, horrible period of insomnia. I bit my lip until it nearly bled, and I shivered.

Finally–finally–Harvey nodded his defeat and turned to walk back toward the car. He climbed inside and firmly closed the door–just hard enough to appear confident, not hard enough to convey annoyance.

"What happened out there?" I hissed through my teeth. "What took you so long?"

With the relief of a scene played out well, at least in his mind, Harvey breathed. His narrowed eyes watched Victor disappear along the stone path between the bushes to our right. Over the bushes we could both see the office door open and close.

"Why don't you drive around the block and wait for me?" he suggested. "I want to sneak back and listen."

"Oh, no," I blurted. "That's much too dangerous."

Harvey's eyes flashed daggers at me. "Victor is probably on the phone calling Luis right now. I'm going back to listen at the window. Unless you want me to get caught, I suggest you take the car around the block."

I considered this new Harvey, this monster of my creation whose reckless soul would forever weigh on my conscience. I considered all that, and still I couldn't find the courage to deflate him.

"Alright, already," I caved in. "Stop at that last bush so we can't be seen."

Harvey parked, then stepped quietly out of the car onto the grass and removed his flip-flops, the better for sneaking up on Victor. I unfolded myself from the back and climbed behind the wheel.

"When you're ready," I said, pointing toward the

white spire poking out above the trees, "head for the church over there. I'll be in the parking lot."

The Spanish teacher's crooked smile reminded me of a boy aiming a slingshot.

"One more thing." I stage-whispered.

"What?"

"Break a leg."

Harvey's grin nearly stretched to his ears.

To ease the car the rest of the way out of the drive I had to turn away from Harvey. When I was able to glance back toward the house, all I could see was a tiny patch of turquoise golf shirt inching toward the nearest office window.

Three minutes later I found the shady spot where Linda had left her car when she spied on Karl.

Naturally I was too nervous to wait in the Subaru, so with a quick glance toward the minister's house (nobody appeared to be home), I set off along the property lines through the trees. I had to skirt a fence or two, but mostly it was easy going, just ducking around shrubs, swatting a pine branch now and then.

Soon I arrived at the edge of Karl's back yard, the scene of the crime; and there I stopped. First of all, I didn't want Victor to notice me cross all the open space. But to be honest the thought of Karl's throat being clamped closed by a pit bull brought the taste of bile to my mouth.

And then I saw him. Harvey the Magnificent. He was trotting along barefoot through the grass like the lover in a perfume commercial.

"You scared the hell out of me," I told him when he joined me under the trees.

He just puffed and hopped from foot to foot while he put his flip-flops back on his feet.

"So?" I prompted.

"It was great. It was really, really great."

"I'm so glad you're happy. Now will you please tell me what happened?"

"Honestly. I've never done anything like that before in my life."

"You're welcome," I said. "Now tell me what happened before I have to hit you."

"Okay, okay." We proceeded slowly, Harvey trying to collect enough lung power to talk, me trying not to make any sound that would cause me to miss a word.

"I got the cousin connection right away," the teacher said, pausing to puff. "I told Victor I read something about his brother, Luis, and he corrected me."

"He actually told you Luis was his cousin?"

"Yes."

"Wonderful!" And then I thought about that. "So you could have left right away! What the hell took you so long?"

"Are you going to listen? Or do you still want to play mother?"

I clamped my mouth shut.

"So," Harvey continued. "So I went into a story about you being my stepsister and how you mentioned him–Victor–and how I made the connection with Luis from the newspaper."

"You mentioned me?"

"He asked how I got his name. And who else do I know who knows him?"

I saw Harvey's point, but I grunted and frowned anyway.

The transformed Spanish teacher continued. "Then I said I've been wanting to see some dog-fight action ever since I was in Mexico and wouldn't he please, please put a good word in with his cousin?"

I shook my head and muttered, "I still wish you'd left

right away."

Harvey stepped around a compost enclosure and tossed me a scowl. "I didn't dare–he was far too suspicious of you."

I took my time skirting the compost, but Harvey didn't notice.

"Was that why you wanted to listen at the window?" I asked. To see if I was in line for the next savage accident?

"Couldn't you see how steamed he was? I knew he'd pick up the phone the second we were gone."

"Which he did."

"Right." Harvey paused to push a pine branch out of his face.

"What did you hear?"

"An argument, of course. One side of an argument anyway. Victor really doesn't trust you much."

My throat ached from thinking about that. I had not guessed, but I realized now that Victor's distrust was logical. Before Karl's death I hadn't visited Linda at all. Since then, I'd been asking questions bound to make a guilty person nervous. If I had suspected Victor sooner, I probably would have taken care to be a little less conspicuous.

I began to twitch again, and I thumped Harvey's arm with my knuckles. "What else?" We rounded a backyard fence and hurried through a small expanse of open space.

"He was talking to his cousin, of course. Trying to convince him to hold off a dog fight that's supposed to take place tonight."

"Tonight!" I shrieked. If I was bursting before, now I absolutely detonated. "Where?" If I could alert the police to the location, they could nab Luis in the act of committing a crime. Depending on how many dogs he owned, the one responsible for Karl's death might even be there!

"Fairmount Park," Harvey answered. "Behind one of the neglected mansions."

The back of my neck prickled. "You're sure Victor didn't talk him into canceling?"

Harvey paused beside a pyracantha bush. "I wasn't entirely clear on all the words," he admitted, "the closed window and all, and classroom Spanish and colloquial Spanish aren't always the same..."

"Don't get all wishy-washy on me now, Harvey. Just tell me what you think you heard."

He jiggled his head, then looked into my eyes. "It sounded like the fight is a championship or something. One match for all the marbles, you know? That's why I think Luis refused to change it. He'd lose face in a big way."

I reached up to lock Harvey in a congratulatory hug, brief, platonic, and totally irrepressible. "You did great," I said into his ear. "Absolutely great. And now I have to hurry up and tell the police." When I pulled away, he was pink all the way down to his bumpy toes.

Rip's car was at hand, and we parted to open our respective doors. Before getting in, however, Harvey patted the Mercury's roof to make me look his way. His face looked like Garry's when he expected to be shot down.

"What?" I prompted.

"Mind if I come along?" Harvey almost begged. "I've never been to a police station."

I could believe it.

"Sure," I said. What the heck?

Chapter 27

I USED MY cell phone to call the office number of the Philadelphia police. After I finally reached someone who knew where the man in charge of Karl's murder investigation was, it took several minutes of explanatory pleading for her to reveal the information. At first "urgent" was interpreted as "emergency." Then "important information" must have come across as "whacko crank." But finally I was given directions to Detective Craig Mansfield's favorite gym, where he was using a late lunch break to work out.

Before Harvey could pout, I explained that the informal setting was much better for my purposes. "Less embarrassing if he doesn't like what he hears."

Of course, I was counting on Mansfield to embrace my theory as spontaneously as I had embraced Harvey when he told me about tonight's dog fight, but experience had taught me that professionals are much more circumspect when listening to private citizens–no matter how well-informed or well-meaning we might be.

Harvey settled his hands contentedly in his lap for the ride into the city. We both smelled a bit gamey from our recent adventure spying on Victor de la Nuez, causing the inside of Rip's car to feel quite intimate. Never again would I spot the broad-shouldered Spanish teacher across a room and wonder whether I would be able to dredge up his name before I needed it. We practiced giving each other friendly smiles all the way to a parking space on the street outside the gym.

The neighborhood was very inner-city with grimy old buildings scrunched together and weeds struggling in yards no bigger than a cow's grave. The lobby of the gym contained a desk centered on a patch of industrial carpet. Off to the left the spacious fitness facility was visible through glass imbedded with chicken wire.

None of the men using the equipment were familiar to me, so I said, "Detective Mansfield?" to the youngster behind the desk. He jerked a thumb toward the snack shop to our right.

The policeman was already back in his sport coat and slacks, hastily stuffing his square, jowly face with a pita-bread sandwich spilling over with something pink and white. Shrimp salad, perhaps. His face was still wet with Old Spice aftershave, and the scent fought with the smell of coffee and unidentifiable food.

At the sight of Harvey in his baggy tan shorts and flip-flops—and me—the cop's mouth dropped open. Autopsies apparently were ho-hum, but stray women and their Spanish-teacher sidekicks showing up at his health club left the detective speechless.

"May we sit down?" I asked. "I have some information that may be of interest."

Mansfield gestured toward two empty patio-style chairs. Only two other patrons occupied the small room, dining separately, oblivious to anything but their food.

"Yuh?" the detective prompted through a mouthful as soon as Harvey and I were settled.

"I have a lead on the dog that might have killed Karl Vogel."

"Yeah?" Only moderate curiosity.

"I found out that Victor de la Nuez's cousin, Luis, was arrested a month or so ago for dog fighting in North Phil-adelphia."

"So?"

"So, Victor de la Nuez worked for Karl. In fact, he still takes care of his house."

"So?"

"So, Luis has another fight scheduled for tonight, and I thought..."

"When tonight?"

"Just before dark," I said, and Harvey nodded his confirmation.

"Where?" The detective reached into a pocket for a small pad and a pen, his studied indifference replaced by a businesslike demeanor. If not for a slight sparkle in his eye, I still would have thought he was more interested in finishing his shrimp salad.

I gestured for Harvey to take it from there. He fidgeted on his seat and spoke to the table. "Well, I told Ginger it was a little difficult to follow, what with the window being closed and the colloquial Spanish and all, but it sounded like Fairmount Park. Behind an old mansion that's a mess." He related the name.

"The park," Mansfield grunted, running his eyes up and down Harvey's torso. "You sure that's what he said?"

"Pretty sure. Why?"

"Because they usually hold 'em in somebody's basement. Less noise, you know? But maybe nobody's takin' a chance after the last raid. Humph." He sat back in his chair and discarded the pen while he regarded both of us. "Sweet." He smiled with departmental self-congratulation.

"It sounded like some sort of championship. That was why Luis refused to cancel."

"Grudge match," Mansfield nodded, perking up. "One fight." He pinched his lower lip between his fingers and stared out the lunchroom's door. "That makes a little more sense."

"You'll check it out?" I asked just to make sure.

"Oh, yeah. We'll show up. It ain't easy catching 'em in the act; and you know this much, you probably know that's what we have to do. So, sure, we'll check it out. But..."

His face regarded his lunch plate with consternation, so I finished for him.

"...but you don't see what this has to do with Karl's death."

Mansfield met my eyes but kept his distance. Maybe he saw. Maybe he didn't. Regardless, the stance he had selected was, "Hands off, amateurs. Leave this to the pros." Otherwise we might somehow manage to mess everything up.

I stood, scraping back my chair noisily on the linoleum. "Come on, Harvey. I'll give you a ride home."

Harvey reluctantly rose. Then he stuck out his hand, forcing Mansfield to do the same. I thought the detective emitted a bit of a belch while he pumped Harvey's arm, but it could have been his chair, too.

Harvey glowered all the way back to the car. For heat relief he left his door open even after he flopped down in the passenger's seat. "Do they always treat you like that?"

Always? What had he heard about me?

"What do you mean?"

"Like they can't decide whether to pat you on your head wish they could shoo you away? I heard you mix it up with the police now and then. Do they always treat you like that?"

I considered evading the question, but I was too tired and too irritated myself. "They're usually polite about it, but yes." 1 admitted. You don't wear a uniform, your information is suspect. Even after I solved my first murder, my old elementary school acquaintance, George Masterson Mills, seemed reluctant to praise my accomplishment. "Quite helpful," was as far as he went. Of course, he might have been afraid I would interfere again if I got the chance.

"Mansfield isn't going to get what you want, is he?" Harvey observed.

I thought about that. On one hand, the detective needed any evidence he could get that would solve Karl's murder. On the other hand, what did he care which dog was responsible when he had a dog-trainer for a suspect?

"Actually, I don't know," I told Harvey as he pulled his door shut and I turned on the engine. Mansfield might not even go to the park himself, and I certainly didn't think anyone else would check whether one of the dogs had a missing claw and a broken tooth. I tried to imagine the scene–excited people hanging on the action, handlers goading their dogs into a frenzy, police rushing in–pandemonium.

"Out of our hands," I said with a shrug.

I asked Harvey where he lived, and he mentioned an apartment building near the Philadelphia Museum of Art and the Franklin Institute.

"Hummm," I said, the location having suggested a slight detour.

Why not? I thought. Nobody had to know.

"How about taking the long way home?" I said flirtatiously.

Harvey raised an eyebrow.

"Through the park."

Harvey smiled.

Since Harvey lived almost across the river from the part of the vast Fairmount Park Victor had mentioned during his argument with Luis, I drove to the right vicinity, then asked my passenger to guide me through the unfamiliar expanses of the park itself.

Heat waves shimmered off the pavement. Gold and silver highlights gilded the green contours of the closely mown grass. Clusters of century-old trees stirred limply with the occasional breeze.

Across an interior road an elderly dog-walker shuffled along wearing what looked like bedroom slippers, her pug-nosed Pekinese following on a slack leash. On the crest of the largest hill two young women sunbathed in tank tops and shorts. The young man sitting against the trunk of an oak alternately read from a textbook and eyed the women. At the edge of the parking lot where I stopped, a businessman spoke into a cell phone while gazing at the broad vista of green.

"This way," Harvey said decisively. He flip-flopped off toward the broadest expanse of grass, away from the half-empty parking lot. Some of the car owners must have been exploring like Harvey and me, for there were more cars than people in sight.

After ten minutes of walking in silence, my blouse stuck to my skin and my bangs were stringy wet. Harvey, too, was flushed from exertion.

We had rounded a boarded-up house, perhaps turn-of-the-century gray-shingled chic, currently a dark monstrosity with "NO TRESPASSING" signs at every possible entrance. Nobody could manage even a peek through a window without a crowbar or an ax, but I supposed some people had nothing better to do.

We had just passed some bushes that appeared to be on steroids, a huge rose of Sharon and some thick decorative pines, when Harvey suddenly stopped. "There," he said. "What do you think?"

Spread before us was a low point in the lawn, a natural amphitheater mostly cut off from its surroundings by dense, overgrown trees and shrubs. Back here the park maintenance staff had failed to mow in recent weeks, perhaps as a natural discouragement to wanderers. Chickweed languished thirstily. Plantain weeds held brown heads high on their tough stems and probably stuck between Harvey's toes when he walked. Dandelions in bloom and past the puff stage proliferated. Gnats hovered in the sunlight and occasionally swarmed our faces.

"Hey!" I shouted into the sky. "Anybody home?" I trotted downhill until I was in the middle of the stage area, perhaps thirty yards from Harvey. "Arf, arf," I barked even louder than when I had tried to intimidate Gretsky from the coffee table.

Harvey, too, ignored my alpha-dog imitation. He stuffed his hands into his baggy pants pockets and sauntered down to join me. "Lucky nobody's within half a mile of here," he remarked, "or I'd be in big trouble with your husband."

"We certainly don't need any trouble with my husband."

Harvey smiled tolerantly. "You don't always tell him what you're doing, do you?"

That brought me up short, I must say. So much so that I worded my answer with great care.

"I don't like to worry him. I'm pretty sure he does the same for me."

"Must be nice," the Spanish teacher reflected.

I did a quick check for the slightest sign of jealousy; not everyone is pleased to discover you have a marriage that works. So far as I knew, Harvey was single and content to be so, but how could I be sure?

His smile withheld nothing, so I grinned back for the appropriate length of time. Funny. Half a day ago Harvey and I scarcely knew each other. But already I'd seen the guy at his best, behavior-wise; and he'd seen me at my worst, if you only considered appearances. If that wasn't friendship material, I didn't know what was.

By tacit agreement we strolled up toward the far side of the natural depression until we stood about seventy yards from the back of the old mansion. Now that we were closer, I could see a couple paths through the underbrush at the base of the far trees. A few feet beyond them seemed to lie a parking area for some maintenance vehicles, an equipment shed, and a covered pile of sand.

"Access by car," I told Harvey when I re-emerged

from the thicket. "It's perfect, isn't it?" I said, knowing Harvey knew I meant, "perfect for a dog fight."

He glanced around, noting the seclusion, the natural sound barriers, the avenues of escape through woods and across fields.

"I'm afraid so," he agreed.

The sun slipped behind a scrawny cloud long enough for a cool shadow to pass over us. I cringed, thinking of the violence to come. "Let's get the hell out of here," I said, and Harvey nodded grimly.

Seventeen minutes later I stopped at the curb next to his apartment building. "Thanks," I told my new compatriot as he stepped out onto the sidewalk.

When he leaned down to speak through the opened window, he looked world-weary, but serene. "It was...interesting," he said. "Let me know how things turn out."

After forty minutes of Friday-afternoon expressway traffic, I finally arrived at home.

Right away Gretsky guilted me into playing catch out back, with two pauses for the primitive necessities. Then I fed him and watered him and we watched each other while he ate. His golden-red ears flopped back and forth while he chewed, and it occurred to me that with a little more gold and a little less red they might have been my twin ponytails back in third grade.

When he was finished, I sat on the kitchen floor and allowed him to mug me with affection—good for elevating my mood, but another reason to take a shower.

Unfortunately, when I was all cleaned up I still felt down. The kids and Rip would be at school all night, involved with water pistol fights and plastic horseshoes, hot dogs over a charcoal grill, hide-and-seek after dark, ghost stories, and toasted marshmallows. Also, cuts and scrapes from tripping over tent stakes, petty damage to the school's equipment, food ground into the lobby carpet–that sort of thing. In the morning everybody would be dirty and irritable from lack of sleep–and I wished with all my heart I was there instead of alone at home brooding over whether Detective Mansfield had taken my suggestions seriously.

But brooding I was and brooding I would be until I did something about it. While I ate my own dinner, I decided to call a doctor about my depression.

Dr. Mathias Fleming listened to my concerns about Mansfield and the dog fight without remark. Then he said, "I've never seen a dog fight, have you?"

"No," I admitted. "You wanna?"

"Be ready in fifteen minutes."

"I'll be there."

For my outing I chose an ensemble of jeans and sneakers (big surprise) and a lightweight long-sleeved blouse to discourage mosquitoes. The event had been called for late twilight, after all. I also doused my wrists, ankles, and neck with Deep Woods Off and brought some along for Doc. He struck me as the Einstein type–somebody who could explain the whole world yet fail to remember his own phone number.

This theory was borne out by Doc's outfit–khaki slacks, another short-sleeved white shirt, and a paisley bow tie. With his wavy white hair, heavy glasses, and wedge of facial wrinkles he appeared to be the consummate, clueless, absent-minded professor–and I was thrilled to my socks that he agreed to accompany me to the dog fight. Taking a noisy, cowardly Irish setter to spy on a championship pitbull battle would have been beyond crazy.

"What's in the bag?" I inquired, for my detection partner carried a lunch bag with something heavy inside.

"I'm an optimist," he said, but no more. Just, "Fill me

in on developments."

All the way to the same parking lot I'd used only a few hours before I performed yet another update.

"Wonderful," Doc Fleming concluded. "I feel lucky tonight. Do you?"

Lucky to have him along. Lucky I wasn't Linda, with her freedom quite possibly in the hands of me and my elderly Lothario...

"Yes, I suppose I do."

Chapter 28

WHEN WE EMERGED from the Subaru, the sky was fading to powder blue. Three boys skateboarded past us along the sidewalk paralleling the park road. A couple strolled across the grass.

And two lone men with furtive eyes scanned the area before setting off toward the dilapidated mansion.

"Right on time," Doc remarked. "We better get ourselves back there. Lead the way." With him he carried the lumpy lunch bag, but before I could ask about the contents, he began a monologue about dog fights I chose not to interrupt. He spoke quite softly, so it was necessary for me to walk close to his side.

"The dogs are all mastiff types," he began. "Larger now than they used to be because of crossbreeding with the dogo Argentino and the Canary Island dog. Still they're matched by weight like our boxers–lightweight, middleweight, heavyweight. Lightweights might range from thirty-five to forty pounds, heavyweights maybe forty-five to fifty. And they keep underground books on them, too."

I asked what that meant.

"Performance records to help set the odds."

"Oh," I said, "then the dogs must fight more than once." I had been imagining horrible mutilating battles until death.

"Yes. A good dog might be worth between $1000 and $4000, so the owner will concede when it's clear who's winning. Then they'll nurse their dogs back to health themselves." Doc spoke with animation and I found myself getting keyed up, too.

"How do you know all this?" I asked as we came within forty yards of the old mansion.

"Speaking to various anticruelty agents in the course of my work."

"Then do you specialize in...this?" So close to the proposed location of the fight, I didn't dare say the word "dog" aloud.

"No, no. Just a sideline. But one that gets me around a bit. It will be interesting to finally see one. It's a felony, you know, just to be there." For a horrible instant I imagined Stevie Luckenbill bailing *me* out. Yet my companion remained confident and eager, so I dismissed the idea. Perhaps Doc was counting on his standing with the court to excuse our presence. Good enough for me.

He paused to ask where I thought we should stand.

This afternoon when Harvey and I were there, I'd noticed a nice dense clump of tree-studded shrubbery on the right lip of the amphitheater just behind the mansion. Playing children or secretive lovers had cleared a spot on the ground that afforded a view of the mansion's back yard. I took Doc by the hand and led him the long way back, away from the more direct route the first arrivals had used.

Already a few men loitered down in the hollow like day-workers waiting for a bus. Although they were still fifty yards away, Doc and I settled cross-legged in our little outdoor closet as quietly as humanly possible. The spot smelled earthy, and I had to relocate a couple of pine cones before I could sit. The ground felt cool and slightly damp.

"Should have brought a blanket," I whispered.

"Shhh," Doc scolded.

During the next half hour more young men of assorted ethnic backgrounds gathered in the clearing. Some seemed to be friends, most not. Only two brought women along.

Gradually, the crowd of about forty or fifty divided

itself more or less into two clusters, probably indicating which dog of the two prospective champions each spectator favored. So far, no dogs were in sight.

A man wearing black slacks and a black shirt wove in and out of the groups taking money and writing bets in a small notebook. Another young man with the air of a bodyguard followed along. When he glanced our way, both Doc and I held our breath.

Darkness was rapidly claiming the park. Fireflies had begun to rise from the grass. Dampness settled around us, and I noticed Doc rubbing his bare arms for warmth.

"You okay?" I whispered.

"Certainly," he replied.

Suddenly two men, one leading a dark brindle pit bull with a white face and bib, stamped through the far edge of growth. "Owner and corner man," Doc explained as the first competitors eased in among the cluster of bettors on the left.

"Remarkable shoulder muscles," I remarked, referring to the dog.

"Treadmill," Doc said. Then, noticing my confusion, he added, "They train them on treadmills."

Soon, also coming from the direction of the maintenance yard, two new men brought a light-tan dog into the clearing. The one leading the dog had a dark Hispanic appearance. Although he was shorter and stockier than Victor, I assumed this was his cousin, Luis.

Murmurs of excitement rose from the crowd, quickly settling down into a buzz. Then everything shifted into double speed, the banker taking bets, the bodyguard's surveys of the fans, the crowd's exclamations. "Hey, Satan, you can take him." "Kill him, Ghost." "You can do it, Ghost."

"Heavyweights?" I asked Doc over the growing noise.

"Probably," he agreed.

The dogs strained for each other. Humans meant nothing to them, but the proximity of another animal inspired hatred. Their gaits were taut with aggression. Their eyes flashed. They barked their threats and growled their intentions. Inexplicably, their tails wagged.

By now my senses tingled with horrible anticipation, which was probably why I could feel someone approaching us from behind–about twenty feet away, moving in with caution.

I didn't stop to think–just moved. With my least visible hand I tugged my blouse out of my waistband. With the other I reached behind Doc's head and pulled his face smack up against mine. I also managed to loosen Doc's ridiculous bow tie.

"Oopfh," the elderly forensic pathologist muttered as he attempted to reclaim his personal space.

No dice. Totally under the influence of fear, my hand-clamp on Doc's neck remained amazingly rigid, permitting only the slightest of withdrawals on his part–just enough for me to notice the whites of his eyes. Our noses touched.

"Kiss me," I hissed. "Hurry up."

The approaching man finally stepped into Doc's peripheral vision, and my very own Einstein made a swift and wholly accurate calculation. Before I knew it, I was draped over his arm receiving a liplock that rivaled my husband's the night he got blitzed on Singapore Slings.

"Hey," said the intruder. "You come on outta dare."

My heart hammered painfully. It seemed a year since I had taken a whole breath. While I corrected that, Doc addressed the man, who I now recognized as the bodyguard who had been following the banker. He was tall and golden, reminding me of the Oscar award on steroids. "What do you want?" Doc asked calmly.

"I want you two outta dare," replied Oscar.

Doc graciously helped me to my feet.

The bodyguard crossed his arms tighter and wrinkled his handsome nose with disgust. "What is dis?" he asked.

Doc and I glanced at each other. We appeared to be mad, passionate lovers about two generations off.

"Jeez," said the intruder. "Canna you take it to a motel?"

"No, my dear man," Doc replied seriously, "we can't."

Then to my horror, he stepped forward and turned Oscar by his arm, leading the thug a few feet away. I busied myself wiping sweat off my palms and tucking in my blouse while Doc spoke man-to-man to the guy. Now and then one of them would steal a glance back at me, so it wasn't very hard to figure who they were talking about. *What* they were talking about was another matter.

Just then the crowd noise rose another decibel. A ringmaster/referee type seemed to be addressing the crowd. During a respite Oscar clapped Doc on the arm and said, "Okay, pops, but stay da hell outta da way."

Doc dragged in a huge breath, but otherwise he remained amazingly composed. The lipstick on his mouth detracted from his dignity, but he swiped it away with a handkerchief. Then he ducked back under the bushes to retrieve his lunch bag.

"What did you say to that guy?" I whispered as we made our way halfway down the hill.

"That you were a thrill seeker, and I was having trouble keeping you interested."

"He believed that?" Yes, I guess he did.

"So, what's in the bag?" I asked after we selected a spot with a good view of the whole scene. Oscar had already trotted back to guard the banker; and the handlers, or cornermen, or whatever they were, had begun to clear the center of the "ring."

"Cheese," Doc answered, eyes on the crowd, his cleaned-up face perfectly deadpan.

My mouth dropped open, but no words emerged. The frenzy just yards away intensified. His arm draped across my shoulders–for verisimilitude–Doc and I watched over the heads of most of the crowd as the dogs' owners held their animals back-to-back by the scruffs of their necks. Feet prancing, backs bristling, the pit bulls growled and yapped and struggled to turn toward each other. Their bone-numbing noises pierced the semi-darkness of the park. Much louder than my own shouting earlier in the day, I wondered whether the raucous sounds reached any ears other than those within sight. Those of the police, for instance.

By now the crowd bristled nearly as much as the dogs being restrained. Fists clenched, the spectators shouted encouragement to their choices–Satan and Ghost. Rabid, vicious, vicarious violence, it sounded almost identical to the crowd at any prize fight.

The fireflies had risen almost to the trees; darkness would be swift. Luis and his rival owner turned their dogs to face each other, holding each high on its hind legs. I stopped breathing until the men let go. Then my lungs filled with a gasp. Instantly, the dogs lunged and arched toward each other's throats. Paws grappled for leverage. My stomach clenched painfully, souring my mouth.

A man shouted, "Don't anybody move," through a bullhorn. Spectators bellowed and scattered, only to encounter Philadelphia police and PSPCA Humane Police Officers brandishing control sticks. Two of the city's trucks rolled across the grass to block further escape. I noticed a couple of knives drop to the ground.

Some bettors got away. Most did not. Everywhere handcuffs snapped onto wrists pulled behind backs.

And the dogs didn't even notice. Satan was down on his back with Ghost at his throat. I heard the pale dog's low, rumbling snarls even through the human shouts and protests. Horrible, nightmare sounds.

Doc and I stayed put, waiting our turn while the police went after the movers. We were able to watch the PSPCA officers wrestle Ghost to the ground in an amazingly swift version of the dominance down. Each dog was tranquilized with an injection. Even after Ghost's body sagged, he maintained his grip on Satan's throat.

Suddenly Doc grabbed my arm and propelled me into the fray. In and out we wove through several tableaus before reaching the officers dealing with the dogs. As we arrived, a man wearing brown slacks and a white shirt with the state emblem on the sleeve passed a four-foot-long flat stick between Ghost's clenched teeth. Satisfied his "break stick" was even left and right, the officer jerked up with one hand and down with the other, effectively separating Ghost's jaws.

Doc touched the man's arm, held out a paper he had brought from his shirt pocket.

"Not now," said the officer.

"Now," Doc insisted with enough force for the man to turn.

"I'm a forensic pathologist working on a murder case, as this letter will confirm, and I have reason to believe this dog killed a man. Before you remove the animal, I'd like to take an impression of his bite to be used as evidence."

The PSPCA officer stood and squinted at the letter, a difficult task because very little daylight remained.

"Oh, hell, go ahead."

"Thanks," Doc said, while glancing around. "Also," he tapped the man's arm, then pointed toward Luis, who was being led toward one of the trucks. "That man, name of Luis de la Nuez, is implicated in the murder. Make sure he stays incarcerated until Detective Craig Mansfield is notified."

"Sure thing, Dr. Fleming. Anything else we can do for you?" The sarcasm was thick, but Doc ignored it.

"Yes. Sign this evidence slip. I'm going to subpoena you for the trial."

The Humane Police Officer rolled his eyes as he reached for Doc's pen.

At last Doc extracted what was indeed a wedge of cheese from the lunch bag. Colby, to be specific. Firm but not crumbly, Doc later explained. He proceeded to use it to get an impression of Ghost's teeth, including a broken upper left canine. Later he would no doubt make a more durable casting to use in court.

While Doc was preoccupied with Ghost's mouth, I checked to see whether one of the dog's front claws was missing.

It was.

Chapter 29

ABOUT TEN the next morning the Barnes family was gathered around the plank table more or less eating cereal.

The campers' parents had been instructed to collect their kids at nine A.M. Saturday morning, the threshold hour for the valiant souls who had supervised the overnight. Apparently the last little darling had fallen asleep playing cards around three and the first little darling awoke when daylight set her tent aglow in shades of neon pink.

Chelsea wore a zombie stare complete with dark bags under her eyes and chalky cheeks. Nearing the bottom of her bowl of Cheerios, she sagged closer and closer to the milk on a fist not quite up to supporting her head.

If possible, Garry was in worse shape. His whole face looked swollen from fatigue. Also, he was eating bran flakes instead of Frosted Flakes and didn't seem to notice the difference.

Rip drank black coffee and sighed heavily from time to time. All three of them would be tucked in and asleep before I finished loading their breakfast dishes into the dishwasher.

This suited my plans perfectly, for I had business to conclude. First a few phone calls in the privacy of Rip's empty office, including one to arrange a final visit with Linda.

When I arrived at her house, shortly after one, she threw her arms around me. "It's finished!" she exclaimed. "How can I ever thank you?"

She looked beautiful with joy. Dressed in faded jeans with a silvery moss-green shirt, I realized I'd never seen her look better.

"Come in, come in," she cooed, tugging eagerly at my

arms. "Oh, Gin. I feel like we're back in high school. Don't you?"

"Not really," I admitted, remembering how we were with each other then.

"You're right. This is better. Now, how about coffee? Tea? I know—champagne. We need to celebrate."

Her effusiveness embarrassed me, so I declined.

"Anything? Please let me fuss over you a little. I have so much to thank you for. Tibor's actually coming home. Did you hear?"

"That's great." I had not known, but it seemed about time for his quarantine to end, and of course the dog had been proven innocent.

I smiled, pleased by the news, then I settled onto Linda's fluffy red sofa while she rummaged around in the kitchen, soon returning with two glasses and a green bottle trimmed with gold foil. "In case you change your mind," she said, referring to the second glass.

I smiled and laughed. Her exuberance was infectious. "Imagine Victor hating Karl enough to kill him like that." She paused in the process of removing the gold foil, the better to shake her head and shiver.

"It is hard to imagine," I agreed, especially when I remembered how grateful Victor had been over Karl helping him to become a United States citizen. Even harder after I spoke to Harvey again.

While she worked on the champagne bottle, Linda stood between the sofa and the opened French doors. I turned to glance outside and found her watching me. Tiny creases of concern caused by the sarcasm in my voice arched above her eyebrows.

"Still, the way he shied away from the police," she went on, "the way he torched my car..." She clucked and shook her head and kept twisting off the wire that encased the cork.

"No," I said.

"What?"

"Victor didn't torch your car."

Linda froze. Then she fluttered a hand and frowned. "That's ridiculous. Victor hated Karl. He thought I would figure it out about him and his cousin, so he tried to kill me. He just got the timing wrong."

"No, Linda, nothing went wrong. You bombed the car." The police said a small, portable TV run on batteries had been loaded with explosives, then detonated with a powerful remote control. They were already busy tracking down the sources of the components. After they learned who the culprit was, that particular chore would become much easier.

Linda's pink lips formed an O of shock. Her eyebrows shot up and she threw the champagne bottle onto an overstuffed chair. It bounced and rolled onto the floor, jarring the silence but remaining intact.

"How could you even think something like that?" Linda spat.

If she really wanted an answer, I could have offered several. The dominance-down maneuver for one. Killing Karl gave her the upper hand permanently, an outcome much more in keeping with her character than the nonsense she fed Bedoes and me about love.

Sadly, my own painful past with Linda also pointed toward her guilt. Spending time with the adult had revived my memories of the teenager, especially the spoiled, I-can-get-away-with-anything arrogance reinforced for so many years by her father's blind approval.

Forced to endure an especially nasty, drawn-out divorce, Linda's life-long scorn for society's conventions defied restraint. Except for the threat of jail time, I had no doubt she would have enjoyed wringing Karl's neck with her very own hands.

Putting the remote-control bomb together with the way Linda once hid behind my innocence, it was easy to conclude the murder had been contracted out. To her it would be a poetic revenge she could enjoy well into her dotage. If she got away with it.

"But Victor..." she began.

"Stuck in the middle. No doubt he's suffering an agony of conscience about now. If he talks, you go to jail and he loses his job. If he doesn't, his cousin takes the primary blame. Either way Victor could be considered an accessory."

I felt sorry for the guy. His absence from the dog fight had caused me to rethink what I knew about him, mainly that he showed up every day for a low-paying, menial job–even after his original employer was dead. Pretty responsible, honest behavior for a supposedly angry, ungrateful man.

Plus Victor told me himself how maligned most of the Cuban refugees had been and, relatively speaking, how few criminals had come over during the Mariel boatlift. Perhaps his cousin was one of the minority, but I doubted very much that Victor was. Especially after I checked with Harvey.

When I had phoned the Spanish teacher this morning, I quizzed him about Victor's attitude and also his exact words. According to Harvey, the thrust of Victor's call to Luis was, "*You're* going to get in trouble. *You* should cancel tonight's fight." Not *"We."* Not *"Us."*

Linda paced, hands on hips, lips pinched together in a defiant scowl. The hardness in her eyes could have chipped diamonds.

"It's nonsense, Gin. Nonsense," she insisted. "Why on earth would I blow up my own car?"

I wanted to scream or throw that ridiculous

champagne bottle against the fireplace, but I held tight to my patience. After all, I was alone with a dangerous woman.

"Because Mansfield had just found your tire tracks in back of the church, remember? They placed you at the scene of the crime."

I'd seen for myself that the parking spot had been in the shade, so I knew the mud could easily have remained damp enough for tire impressions the morning of the murder.

"So now I suppose you're saying Tibor killed Karl after all?"

"No. You hired Luis to use his pit bull." Payment was probably contingent on the Cuban's guarantee of silence. If he kept Linda out of it, he could afford to hire the best defense money could buy. Talk and she'd throw him to the wolves.

"Preposterous."

"Is it?"

"Of course. This is all your wild speculation. Honestly, Gin. You and that imagination of yours have really gone too far. I should probably sue."

I shook my head. "It's the only explanation that makes sense. None of the other people who hated Karl knew Victor–only you. Even if one of the others saw the name Luis de la Nuez in the newspaper, it wouldn't have meant a thing to them." I shook my head again. "I'd say you threatened Victor to get to Luis. Maybe Victor *is* a reformed criminal. Maybe he has some other secret. He's worked for you long enough for you to know him pretty well. Or maybe you just threatened to rat on Luis. Doesn't matter. Whatever blackmail you used to get his cooperation can't possibly be as bad as an accessory-to-murder charge. He'll probably be offered immunity in exchange for his testimony anyhow."

Then no doubt he would describe how Linda scouted out the best time for Luis to make his move, which happened to be while Karl was placing the food out in the yard for Tibor to track. Of necessity, Tibor would have remained in the house while Karl did that. After the attack, Luis would have secured his dog and released Tibor so the German shepherd would be found near the body. Even if instinct hadn't dictated that he lick his master's wounds, he would have appeared guilty–he was the only dog there!

Linda had begun pacing again, pounding her fist into her palm like one of the agitated spectators at the pit-bull fight. "I always hated you," she confessed.

Standing up, I saw the champagne bottle on the floor, too far away to use for protection. Force wasn't my thing anyhow–just ask Gretsky. I went with my strength instead.

"And I always liked you," I said with sorrow. "You shouldn't have used me."

That surprised Linda so much she stopped pacing. "You made such a perfect sycophant," she observed. "Why'd you have to wise up?"

I considered the question. "Actually, you're largely to blame," I concluded.

The way she had treated me for worshiping her back in high school taught me to look long and hard at any potential friends. I wouldn't say I became wary of everyone–too pessimistic for me. Rather I became a realist. My recent relapse had probably been one last attempt to close the lid on Pandora's box.

And, just maybe, I was trying to polish up an old man's image of his daughter one more time.

While Linda smoldered in silence, I took the opportunity to mention that Detective Mansfield was on his way.

Linda's eyes snapped at me, then narrowed. She folded her arms and addressed the ceiling, or perhaps the higher plane where a judge would reside. Angry tears filled her eyes. "When you called my father, I thought it was the luckiest break of my life." Her lip quivered, and she clamped it between her teeth.

I nodded my agreement. Bedoes probably had been pressing her to hire a professional investigator, as well he should have.

"I've always been able to sway Dad," Linda mused. "He couldn't cope with the idea that his little girl wasn't quite as pure of heart as he hoped. When we were kids, he bent over backwards trying to believe I was just like you.

"After you called Dad, I was able to convince him all I needed was someone discreet who cared about me. You, in other words–I was sure you'd bungle it, you know?"

"So why have Bedoes handle me? Why not do it yourself?"

She snorted. "With our history?" Her expression said she wouldn't have responded to a plea from me, and she feared equal treatment. "Nah. I told Tim you were jealous of my money, but you'd probably agree to help if he asked on behalf of my father."

I wagged my head at how easy it all had been.

Someone knocked on the door, and I scurried to answer it before Linda could read the word "sucker" all over my face.

"Hi." Detective Mansfield actually greeted me warmly, a continuation of the sweetness and light he'd bestowed upon me earlier on the phone, my thanks for the dog-fight tip, although the words "thank you" had not yet crept into the conversation. Instead he called Dr. Fleming and me idiots, conceding only that, "Doc does good field work, though."

I chose to set a better example. "Linda Arden," I began in my best textbook manners. "You've met Detective Craig Mansfield. Detective, you remember Linda Arden."

Then, as one should, I added a remark calculated to help the newly reintroduced parties initiate their own conversation.

"Detective," I said, "did you know that Linda hired Luis de la Nuez to kill her husband?"

Apparently, I'd handled the social difficulties okay, because both parties began to talk at once.

I didn't listen. My attention had been drawn to a white envelope with no return address. The forgotten good-luck/ bad-luck chain letter was still on the coffee table where Linda had left it.

Chapter 30

"IT'S SPECIESISM really," Doc said in response to Stevie's remark. They were standing at my stove, the tall, thin, white-haired forensic pathologist (specialty dog bites) and the tiny blond vegetarian animal activist Stevie Luckenbill, who was cooking something in my largest pot. The food consisted of small granules in various earth tones. The steam wafting off it smelled like armpits.

"Exactly," agreed Stevie, waving my big slotted spoon at the world in general. "Just because we know how to dominate all the other animals doesn't mean we should. What if they suddenly grew big brains and decided to treat us that way?"

"Isn't going to happen," Didi butted in as she joined us. I was peeking in the oven at my barbecued spare ribs (the alternative to whatever Stevie was cooking), while also giving my nose a break.

As one, Stevie and Doc turned to stare at Didi, who blinked under their accusing gaze. "Well, it isn't."

"That's not the point!" Stevie sputtered, other words of rebuttal obviously jamming in their rush to exit her mouth.

"What the young lady means," Doc addressed my best friend, "is we all have our place on earth..."

"One big happy family," Didi interjected with a slightly sarcastic nod. She could condemn politics as cynically as any politician.

"...Yes, and it's presumptuous of us–to say the least– to think we're the most important family member just because we're the smartest."

I couldn't help thinking of Tibor and his doomed family. At least the schutzhund champion was now safely in Victor de la Nuez's capable hands. Linda had hired the handyman to look after him and her home indefinitely, a practical arrangement, which also fostered the hope that one day she might return.

Didi's nose wrinkled, either from the information or the odor.

"Do you like horses?" Stevie asked.

Didi shrugged. "What's not to like?"

"Ever hear of Premarin? It's used for hormone therapy for women."

Didi glared her non-reply.

"Well, to make it they confine pregnant mares and restrict their water intake to make their urine stronger. Does that sound fair?"

Didi's mouth opened for another non-answer.

"You have a pet?" Stevie pressed.

Didi shot me a glance because I had requested that Chevy stay home pending completion of her housebreaking. "A dog–Chivas Beagle," she answered. "What about her?"

"Tell me something about her you like."

Didi relaxed her spine, elbows, and knees. Immediately her cotton sundress and sandals looked better. Her face, too, because it got all dreamy.

"I tried something I read in a book–putting a little bell on my back door so Chevy can poke it when she wants to go out. When she comes in, I give her a cookie. Trouble is the little stinker loves those cookies, you know? So all day long it's ding, ding, ding. My house sounds like Macy's at Christmastime."

Didi chuckled and wagged her head in that tolerant parental way we all use when we're disguising a boast in the form of a complaint.

Gretsky entered the kitchen just then and fluffed out his cheeks at me. He was either blowing raspberries sideways or trying to bark without any sound. I glanced at the clock and lo and behold, it was his feeding time.

"See?" Stevie crowed over Gretsky's cuteness. Then she opened the oven and Didi looked in. "What if somebody did this to your dog?"

Didi covered her mouth and ran from the room.

"Hey," I said, scolding Stevie with a scowl. "You live and let live in my house. One big happy family–you got it?"

"Sorry." Stevie's eyes suddenly became teary. Doc touched her shoulder with his hand, and she turned to hide her face in his shirt. Her wet nose must have hit mid-button between his front pocket and his belt.

Doc met my ironic smile with understanding.

Since the dog-fight evening two weeks before, my relationship with him had changed. Now we felt more like coworkers with shared battle experience than grandfather and granddaughter. To me, the difference was an improvement–blind mutual affection had given way to a more equitable mutual respect. On my way out to Didi, it occurred to me to give my mother another shot at him when he returned to testify at the trials. After all, he *was* a hell of a kisser.

Didi had slumped over the picnic table, maybe crying, maybe not. Chelsea, Garry, and Rip occasionally glanced up from their croquet game on the other side of the fence to monitor her emotional state. Didi being Didi, however, none of them allowed her theatrics to spoil their aim.

My dearest friend and confidante lifted her head. Apparently, the tears were real.

"She's right, you know," Didi asserted. "I'll never eat meat again."

"That's pretty extreme. How about just being a responsible carnivore?"

"What's that?" What I was leaning toward. Buying free-range chickens, no veal, much, much less beef, serving meatless meals now and then, I explained.

To no avail. "No can do. Stevie's right."

I sighed. My dramatic friend was an adult, or–put more accurately–she was thirty-four years old. She would do what she would do, and the rest of the world could just plain sit back and watch.

I patted her back, and saved my breath.

As it turned out, nobody ate meat that night. While I was carrying Stevie's concoction out to the picnic table, Gretsky snagged the baking dish of spare ribs off the stove. Glass and barbecue sauce spattered six feet in every direction.

I caught the dog sampling a rib and shrieked at him. Say what you will about meat, I was positive that pork bones and glass were unhealthy for anybody.

Gretsky backed into the entranceway and eyed me with distrust, ears down, eyebrows slanted, feet quivering with readiness for flight.

I controlled my voice, modulated it into a coo. "Easy there," I said.

Gretsky growled a warning. A bone protruded from his mouth.

"Easy there," I said. "You're okay."

I reached for his greasy prize.

Gretsky ran for the family room.

I shut the door behind us. "Down!" I shouted, and he flopped onto his belly. His eyes never left my face. The irritable growling resumed.

"Stay!" I demanded. Quickly, I twisted the brittle pork bone from his teeth. His eyes widened with surprise.

"Good dog," I congratulated him. "You're the best."

Exclamations from the kitchen resounded down the hall into our private conference–Rip and the kids lamenting the loss of our main course.

"Gin?"

"In here."

Rip met me at the doorway, and I handed him the slippery bone.

"Oh," he said, realizing what had just happened. "Why don't you babysit the beast while I clean up the kitchen?" Both of us knew Gretsky would try to scratch down the door if we left him alone.

"Good deal," I replied.

After Rip shut us in together, I sat on the floor facing our four-legged family member. Fearing the worst, he had trouble meeting my eyes.

"What are we going to do with you?" I clucked as I reached out to pet him. Instinctively, Gretsky shrunk back.

When I leaned forward to hug his head and rub his ears, his whole body relaxed. He was forgiven. Hallelujah. He slurped me from chin to cheek.

I sighed with resignation. "Yeah," I admitted. "I love you, too."

#

Dear Reader—**Pretty please!** If you enjoyed NO BONES ABOUT IT, a **brief review** on the product page of whatever online bookseller you prefer would be enormously helpful. <u>Fellow readers will greatly appreciate your advice</u>, *and* it's the easiest way to make an author very, very happy.

Interested in being the first to hear about a special bargain, a new release, a tempting contest, or maybe just some good news? Please join my **email list** (gift involved). Link on my website:
<u>donnahustonmurray.com</u>

Many thanks!

Donna

Acknowledgements

Quite a few fascinating people made this book especially fun for me, and I'd like to thank them profusely for their help. First there's Michelle Argyle of MDA Books, who designed the wonderful new cover. Dr. Claus Peter Speth; Charlene Peters and Humane Police Officer Gary Lovett, from the PSPCA; the Greater Philadelphia Schutzhund Club, Inc., especially Patsy Joyce, Maureen Roberts, and Todd Shilkret; Sgt. Peter Gangl of the Tredyffrin Police; Ed Hill, Head Trainer of the Philadelphia Canine Unit; Marguerite Lencoski, Resident Kennelkeeper at the Francisvale Home for Smaller Animals; and the real Gretsky's friend and veterinarian, Dr. George Jeittles–all were exceptionally generous with their time and information.

Other contributors were Mary Remer, Leah Flocco, Ruth Heston, Claire Satlof and Jeff Bedrick, Norman Mawby, Mike Carroll, Gene Dooley, Dr. Kenneth Zamkoff and Dr. Judith Stein, Paul and Jane Woody, Helen Lane and Ron Longe, Charles Shields, David Moore, and Michele Cesena; and I thank them profusely, too.

Some statistical information was gleaned from Bat Conservation International, Inc., and from the excellent book, *The Animal Rights Movement in America* by Lawrence Finsen and Susan Finsen, Twayne Publishers.

Very special thanks, too, to Ann Landers and Creators Syndicate for granting permission for me to quote from her column.

–Donna

The next Ginger Barnes Cozy Mystery

A SCORE TO SETTLE: When the murder of an NFL quarterback endangers her family, savvy football fan and sometime-sleuth, Ginger Barnes, rushes to Norfolk, VA. Her cousin, Michelle, terrified that her husband will be accused of killing his longtime rival, has been hospitalized to save her pregnancy. No amount of hand-holding or take-out food will do. Gin must tackle the suspicions head-on to save an innocent life.

Chapter 1

"YOU KNOW the doctor only told you to read the sports page because it's so boring, right?" Said as I delivered my husband's toaster waffles. "Box scores and statistics. Who got arrested for mouthing off at a night club. Boorrr-ing."

Rip's blood pressure had been up at his recent physical, so our doctor had written an actual prescription ordering him to read the sports page. Razzing my husband about it was my way of reminding him to slow down and relax.

His eyes tightened as he extended his hand, and I slapped the *Philadelphia Inquirer* onto it with a crooked smile.

To you, Robert Ripley Barnes may be just another forty-two-year old guy in a blue buttoned-down shirt and a patterned tie, but when his cheeks shine with that spicy after-shave and his damp, dark hair looks a little too perfect, I can scarcely resist mussing him up and giving him a really good reason to stay home.

Rarely works. Okay, NEVER works. Apparently, it would be bad form for the Head of School to chastise a teacher for tardiness if he's guilty of it himself. Not for nothing do they say, "It's lonely at the top."

"Just curious," he said as he snapped open the paper. "Did you collect this from the driveway in that outfit?"

Clutching my pink bathrobe closed at the throat, I answered, "Maybe," scarcely above a whisper. Rip's job hadn't moved us to Philadelphia's famously upscale "Main Line" all that long ago, and I guess I was still adapting. Perhaps an overcoat to run out for the paper?

Then again, who was around to care? Certainly not Letty MacNair, the zany recluse next door to our left. Her whole wardrobe improved tenfold when she discovered sweat suits at KMart. And nobody else could even see our driveway through the unkempt bushes and trees that edged our yard.

Still...

"Maybe you should start picking up your own paper," I suggested, but Rip wasn't listening.

"Doc said you wouldn't get it," he groused, abandoning the last of his coffee.

"The paper?"

"The sports page thing. I shouldn't have told you."

"Nonsense," I said, happy to resume the game. "Just because I think it's soap opera fodder doesn't mean..."

"Gin," he interrupted.

"...that you can't read it to your..."

"Gin!" Rip grasped my arm. Then he turned the first page around for me to read.

"TOMCATS' QUARTERBACK FOUND MURDERED," screamed the three-inch headline.

My heart pounded and my mouth went dry. "Doug's dead?" My cousin Michelle's husband. They were expecting their first child in March.

"No, no," Rip said, patting my hand. "I thought that, too. Keep reading."

"Tim Duffy Shot in Stadium Training Room," the subheading clarified.

I couldn't help it; I sighed with relief. Without question, losing Doug would devastate the fragile mother-to-be.

I scanned what little the police had released. "After the Tomcats' 28–20 victory over the Houston Hombres, backup quarterback Tim Duffy lingered in the training room to use the whirlpool...body discovered by a security guard closing up...police theorize that a crazed fan hid in the stadium...no suspects as yet...shocked the sports world...great loss…"

A color photo showed Tim Duffy kneeling with a blue on blue helmet under his arm as he stared off into two-dimensional space. A worldly shrewdness emanated from his shadowed eyes, plus a ruthlessness most ambitious people were wise enough to hide. Otherwise he was just another extremely fit, brown-haired athlete who would never see his thirtieth birthday.

"Too close," I remarked, folding over the paper as our thirteen-year-old approached.

"What's up?" Chelsea asked as she glanced between her father and me. Today's yellow pullover highlighted the nutmeg-colored hair she had inherited from me.

"Teammate of Uncle Doug got shot," Rip answered honestly. Our kids' friends were well aware of the Barnes family's connection to the newest expansion team.

Chelsea's onyx eyes widened and her lips formed a perfect, choir-boy O.

"Wow," our son, Garry, piped up, dropping his

backpack at his sister's heels. Genetics had given him his dad's hazel/green eyes and dark, straight hair. Still only eleven, he was an awkward, ingenuous kid who occasionally came up with astonishingly mature remarks. At the moment I couldn't tell if he was amazed or thrilled by the awful things grown-ups did to each other.

"Where'd it happen?" he asked.

"Training room in Nimitz stadium. Duffy stayed late to use the whirlpool."

"Wow," Garry repeated. "I wonder if Uncle Ronnie was there."

We had been with Michelle's brother, Ronnie Covington, scarcely two weeks ago on Thanksgiving. What had begun the afternoon as a title-of-convenience for Garry had evolved into a gold-plated badge of honor. "My *Uncle* Ronnie is a cinematographer for *NFL Films*!"

Chelsea's thoughts had gone another direction. "Premeditated?" she wondered aloud as she settled onto her chair.

"Not necessarily." Rip cast me a glance that said, "See what your snooping started?"

I sympathized with him. I did. The painfully human problems that crossed a Head of School's desk on a daily basis were enough to make any father protective. But kids needed to develop a sense of justice, too, and a willingness to do the right thing.

"Lots of people carry guns," Garry observed as if it were the most natural thing in the world. "I bet with the big bucks those players earn, they really need 'em, too."

I wanted to dispute my son's logic; but unfortunately, he was probably right. Instead I went to collect waffles for him and put in some for his sister.

Gretsky, our young Irish setter, wandered in, glanced around with proprietary interest, then trotted over to his breakfast. His chewing sounded like footsteps on crushed rock.

To change the subject Rip asked if we wanted to hear the entries for Bryn Derwyn's mascot. In the small private school's brief decade and a half of existence, nobody had agreed on a name for the sports teams, so each coach made up his or her own. The completion of a new gym was the perfect time to correct the problem. Rip, of course, had the deciding vote.

"Do tell," I encouraged him.

Fork in mid-air, he consulted the ceiling as if seeking heavenly intervention. "Dorks, Druids, Banshees, Baby Elephants..." punctuated with the fork.

"You're kidding!"

He swore he was not.

"What else?"

"Dragons, Deer, Dickenses, that by the chair of the English department, of course. The Doldrums, by the faculty at large." It was that time of year, early December. Winter vacation never came soon enough at a school.

"Whatever will you choose?"

Rip shrugged.

"Make one up yourself, Dad," Chelsea suggested.

"Wouldn't be kosher," he muttered as if he were tempted to do exactly that.

Minutes later our kids hurried out to their bus, leaving Gretsky to spin out his frustration in the front hall.

Rip and I cleared dishes in a mutual mood of gloom while the dog tip-toed back and forth between us. Then Rip, too, went to collect his overcoat.

At the front door he grasped my shoulders, looked me in the eye, and said, "You know the murder can't possibly have anything to do with Doug or Michelle." He wiggled my shoulders a little until I lifted my chin. "You know that."

"Yes," I agreed grudgingly, and he pulled me in close.

The phone rang, and Rip released me to reach around

the corner to answer it.

"Hold on," I stalled my husband as he twisted the doorknob. At this hour it was probably a teacher calling in sick, delayed by car trouble, something like that. Yet after the greeting, I covered the mouthpiece and whispered, "It's Ronnie."

Unfortunately, I had already operated as a "concerned citizen" too many times to suit Rip, so a call from that particular cousin right after an NFL player's sensational murder alarmed my mate. I could tell by the flint in his scowl.

"It's about Michelle," I quickly added. Probably something worrisome about the baby judging by Ronnie's voice.

Rip mouthed a silent "Call me at work," then shut the door hard behind him.

As I settled my backside on the kitchen counter and the receiver against my ear, I thought of the Morton's salt slogan, "When it rains, it pours."

Maybe it could be our family motto.

#

For wherever you are and whatever format you like best, you can order from here:
https://books2read.com/u/3nO9lK

Donna Huston Murray's cozy mystery series features an amateur sleuth much like herself, a DIY headmaster's wife with a troubling interest in crime. The latest Gin Barnes novel FOR BETTER OR WORSE was a Finalist for the 2019 National Indie Excellence Award, mystery category, and both books in her new mystery/crime series won Honorable Mention in genre fiction from Writer's Digest.

At home, Donna assumes she can fix anything until proven wrong, calls trash-picking recycling, and although she should probably know better by now, adores Irish setters.

Donna and husband, Hench, live in the greater Philadelphia, PA, USA.

Made in the USA
Las Vegas, NV
13 November 2021